Fandango at the Wall

Fandango at the Wall

CREATING HARMONY BETWEEN THE UNITED STATES AND MEXICO

Foreword by **DOUGLAS BRINKLEY**

KABIR SEHGAL

Music by **ARTURO O'FARRILL** and
THE AFRO LATIN JAZZ ORCHESTRA
with **SPECIAL GUESTS**

Afterword by **AMBASSADOR ANDREW YOUNG**

GRAND CENTRAL
PUBLISHING

NEW YORK   BOSTON

Grand Central Publishing

Hachette Book Group

1290 Avenue of the Americas, New York, NY 10104

grandcentralpublishing.com

twitter.com/grandcentralpub

First Hardcover Edition: September 2018

Grand Central Publishing is a division of Hachette Book Group, Inc. The Grand Central Publishing name and logo is a trademark of Hachette Book Group, Inc.

All song lyrics reprinted with permission.

The publisher is not responsible for websites (or their content) that are not owned by the publisher.

The Hachette Speakers Bureau provides a wide range of authors for speaking events. To find out more, go to www.hachettespeakersbureau.com or call (866) 376-6591.

Print book interior design by Cindy Joy

Library of Congress Control Number: 2018949849

ISBNs: 978-1-5387-4795-7 (hardcover), 978-1-5387-4796-4 (ebook), 978-1-5491-9995-0 (audiobook)

Printed in the United States of America

10 9 8 7 6 5 4 3 2 1

To Jorge Francisco Castillo
and the intrepid organizers of the
Fandango Fronterizo festival

Books by Kabir Sehgal

NON-FICTION

Coined

Jazzocracy

Fandango at the Wall

Walk in My Shoes (with Andrew Young)

Legion of Peace (with Muhammad Yunus)

CHILDREN'S BOOKS

(all with Surishtha Sehgal)

A Bucket of Blessings

The Wheels on the Tuk Tuk

Festival of Color

Thread of Love

P for Poppadoms

Mother Goose Goes to India

POETRY

Home: Where Everyone Is Welcome (with Deepak Chopra)

"I thought of the wilderness we had left behind us, open to sea and sky, joyous in its plenitude and simplicity, perfect yet vulnerable, unaware of what is coming, defended by nothing, guarded by no one."

—EDWARD ABBEY, American novelist

"I do not think there was ever a more wicked war than that waged by the United States on Mexico. I thought so at the time, when I was a youngster, only I had not moral courage enough to resign."

—ULYSSES S. GRANT,

18th President of the United States and general

"I paint flowers so they will not die."

—FRIDA KAHLO, Mexican artist

TABLE OF CONTENTS

FORMATS

This is a multimedia project that comes in multiple formats:

Fandango at the Wall—Book with CD

- Format: Hardcover book with CD. Also available in e-reader versions.

- About: The book is written by Kabir Sehgal. The CD includes four *son jarocho* songs; one piece by Rahim AlHaj Trio; one piece by Sahba Motallebi; and two pieces performed by Arturo O'Farrill and the Afro Latin Jazz Orchestra.

- Availability: all major book retailers

- Publisher: Hachette Audio and Grand Central Publishing

Fandango at the Wall—Complete Music

- Format: Available as a digital download or streaming. Also comes in a two-CD set.

- About: Nearly 30 songs led by Arturo O'Farrill and the Afro Latin Jazz Orchestra. These songs include *son jarocho* pieces that feature the likes of Patricio Hidalgo, Ramón Gutiérrez, Tacho Utrera, Fernando Guadarrama, Wendy Cao, Martha Vega Hernandez, Zenen Zeferino, and Jorge Castillo, among others. The rest of the music features O'Farrill, his band, and special guests such as Regina Carter, Antonio Sanchez, Akua Dixon, Villalobos Brothers, Ana Tijoux, Rahim AlHaj Trio, Mandy Gonzalez, and Jose "Gurri" Gurria-Cardenas, among others. We recorded the music at the San Diego–Tijuana border and also at the Power Station studio in New York City.

- Availability: all major music retailers and streaming services
- Music is a Kabir Sehgal Production.
- Record label: Resilience Music Alliance

Fandango at the Wall—Audio Book

- Format: Digital download
- About: Douglas Brinkley reads the foreword, Kabir Sehgal reads his book and the afterword, which was written by Ambassador Andrew Young. Arturo O'Farrill underscores portions of the reading with a solo piano performance.
- Publisher: Hachette Audio
- Availability: all major book retailers

Fandango at the Wall—Documentary

- Format: film
- This is a work in progress.
- Please get in touch if you want to help at www.kabir.cc.

SONG LIST

The CD that accompanies this book begins with four *son jarocho* songs listed below. These songs feature Patricio Hidalgo, Ramón Gutiérrez, Tacho Utrera, Fernando Guadarrama, Wendy Cao, Martha Vega Hernandez, among others. "Chant" is a song performed by Rahim AlHaj Trio, and "Birth" is a solo piece by Sahba Motallebi. "El Maquech" and "Up Against the Wall" are performed by Arturo O'Farrill and the Afro Latin Jazz Orchestra with special guests.

- El Siquisiri

- El Cascabel

- El Cupido

- La Bamba

- Chant

- Birth

- El Maquech

- Up Against the Wall

The complete music of nearly 30 songs is sold and available separately.

Performing a fandango in Tijuana and looking through the border wall

Son jarocho musicians Patricio Hidalgo, Ramón Gutiérrez, Tacho Utrera (all standing) performing with Arturo O'Farrill and the Afro Latin Jazz Orchestra

FOREWORD

I

When my musician friends Arturo O'Farrill and Kabir Sehgal asked me to co-produce the album *Fandango at the Wall* and write a preface to the book version of the multimedia project, I seized the opportunity. Ever since Donald Trump issued deeply racist and bullying taunts about building an aesthetically ugly 722-mile-long wall along the US-Mexico border, I've hungered to protest. When Ronald Reagan was president in 1986 during the Cold War, he thundered "Mr. Gorbachev, tear down this wall" while in divided Berlin; the world cheered for the triumph of freedom over totalitarianism. Trump, by contrast, wants to build a *huge* border wall, permanently destroying desert ecosystems in California, Arizona, New Mexico, and Texas just to keep Mexicans out of the US. Building a border wall against Mexico has become *the* stark symbol of Trump's anti-immigration stance and Yankee arrogance toward its neighbors in the Western Hemisphere. History won't treat Trump kindly for this grotesque, misguided, xenophobic, and warped fantasy of a Fortress America.

As Sehgal explains in this book, Trump's wall between the US and Mexico is embedded in the politics of trade. If the Mexican government would develop a prosperous economy, undocumented Mexicans wouldn't voluntarily cross the border hungry for work. Instead of promoting the border wall, Trump would be better served by pressing the Mexican government to stomp out systemic corruption. Mexicans are proud of their cultural identity, and if they *could*, they would prefer to stay in the ancient land of the Aztec. Binational relations between our two countries have been moving backward ever since Trump encouraged his supporters to chant "Build that wall!" at rallies. "Oh, we're going to build that wall," Trump reassured them. "Believe me, we're going to build that wall."

Before Trump other US presidents had erected miles of concrete barriers and corrugated steel walls along the border, but euphemistically called it "fencing." Even though boundary stone and GPS data can effectively keep track of border crossings, many Americans have unfortunately clamored for chain link fences and levee walls with bollards. These hyper security measures have engendered human rights protests. One of the very best anti–border wall songs, in fact, was written in 2006 against George W. Bush's retrograde "fence" along the border: It's a finger-pointing ballad by Tom Russell titled "Who's Gonna Build Your Wall?" The song took on fresh relevancy when Trump won the 2016 US presidential election:

> *There's one thing that I most fear*
> *It's a white man in a golf shirt*
> *With a cell phone in his ear*
> *Who's gonna build your wall boys?*
> *Who's gonna mow your lawn?*
> *Who's gonna cook your Mexican food*
> *When your Mexican maid is gone?*
> *Who's gonna wax the floors tonight*
> *Down at the local mall?*
> *Who's gonna wash your baby's face?*
> *Who's gonna build your wall?*

The lyrics to "Who's Gonna Build Your Wall?" are modeled after a real-life San Diego developer who used undocumented Mexican immigrants to build the border wall to keep them from entering California. For Russell there is something perverse about US taxpayers building a border wall instead of rebuilding America's deteriorating infrastructure. "It's a true story," Russell explained. "It's sort of a tongue-in-cheek song, of course. I did it on the *David Letterman Show* years ago. The CBS staff didn't want me to do it, but I told them to ask Dave. Unconcerned about fallout or sponsor's complaints, he told them to let me sing it…and I did."

What Russell understands is that music and satire are powerful weapons in the anti-wall movement. Likewise, this book reminded me anew that shared music between the US and Mexico can be a change agent. Just as rock 'n' roll and jazz helped bring down the Berlin Wall, the power of the *fandango* might derail Trump's boondoggle. This was the altruistic thinking of Sehgal and O'Farrill as they helped organize one of the most innovative musical events in recent US-Mexican history, a multimedia project inspired by Fandango Fronterizo, a festival held Memorial Day weekend in Playas de Tijuana in 2018.

Besides being a brilliant jazz composer, Arturo O'Farrill, a Mexican native and musical prodigy, is one of the top musicologists alive. As the director of the Afro Latin Jazz Orchestra, based in New York City, he eagerly embraces the musical traditions of myriad cultures. Often dressed in loose-fitting guayabera shirts with bright-colored Converse sneakers, O'Farrill has the owlish look of a Mexican musicology professor weaned on the music of Dizzy Gillespie. He is a one-person global jukebox and connoisseur of the *son jarocho* musical traditions from Veracruz, Mexico, which is the heart and soul of this *Fandango* project. The Mexican *jarocho* music O'Farrill taught me about is rhythm-infused, one big jam session for whoever can strum two chords in tune. Much like New Orleans jazz, Veracruz *jarocho* mixes elements of Spanish classical forms with African rhythms brought to Mexico long ago. The *jarocho* style swings and pulsates with high-octane exuberance. The word *jarocho* actually means "brusque" or "out of order" in Spanish. When applied to Veracruz it means dance music that often includes such instruments as *arpa veracruzana* (Veracruz harp), *jarana* (a type of folk guitar), and even virtuoso violin.

As a professor of US presidential history, I will forever associate Veracruz with Woodrow Wilson's unnecessary military intervention in 1913, triggering a seven-year war with Mexico. Even a century later the grim memory of US troops marching through the streets of Veracruz triggers residual anger in Mexico. Warren Zevon, in his album *Excitable Boy*, co-wrote the song "Veracruz" with Jorge Calderón about the tragic US military incursion into the beautiful Gulf of Mexico coastal city from the perspective of a defiant blood-in-his-eyes Veracruz resident. The song begins with this resolute eyewitness proclaiming his hometown love of Veracruz's cultural and spiritual wellsprings.

> *I heard Woodrow Wilson's guns*
> *I heard Maria crying*
> *Late last night I heard the news*
> *That was dying*
> *Veracruz was dying*

Foreword

What didn't get squelched by Woodrow Wilson's brazen intervention of Veracruz was the indigenous music and poetry. In this book Kabir Sehgal, an accomplished jazzologist and composer, recounts the surreal political misunderstandings that occur between these two great democracies with the shared border. His 2008 book *Jazzocracy* had focused on the inter-connectedness between jazz and democracy. Our Grammy Award–winning *Presidential Suite* collaboration brought that philosophy to life with a large ensemble jazz band. For one of the jazz compositions of *Presidential Suite*, I read Reagan's "Tear Down the Wall" speech. In *Jazzocracy* Sehgal proclaims that rhythm is a "Bill of Rights that must be respected," and that the power of jazz grooves are "vested in four equal beats, jazz as a democracy vests power among constituent people." Echoing Plato's *Republic*, there is a wonderful riff in *Jazzocracy* about how music can topple governments and stoke social change.

Sehgal applies his jazz philosophy to the human condition between the US and Mexico in this book. Veracruz, he knows, survived the 1913 US intervention by embracing the Gulf city's time-honored *son jarocho* traditions. Music served as a curative for the cultural rebirth of Veracruz once US forces evacuated. Furthermore, the Veracruz sound deeply influenced the Chicano power movement of the 1970s in East Los Angeles, San Diego–Tijuana, and El Paso–Juarez. In Mexico there have been masters of the style—like José Aguirre Vera, José Aguirre "Cha Cha," and Cirilo Promotor. But my only true appreciation of *son jarocho*, before working with O'Farrill and Sehgal on *Fandango at the Wall*, was through the dance-driven music of Los Lobos, particularly in their adaptation of the traditional "El Canelo."

Throughout the 1970s Los Lobos and other Chicano performers in East Los Angeles brought "folkloric *jarocho* genres" into their fast-paced repertoire. Just as the African American freedom struggle drew inspiration from gospel, blues, and R&B, the combination of *corridos* (narrative folk songs native to the American Southwest and northern Mexican) and *jarocho* energized the Brown Power movement led by heroes of mine like Cesar Chavez, Oscar Acosta, and Dolores Huerta. Back in 1970 *Los Angeles Times* correspondent Ruben Salazar was killed by a police tear gas projectile when he covered the Latino anti–Vietnam War marches. *Corridos* were written to honor Salazar, and Hunter S. Thompson wrote a long eulogistic essay in tribute to his courage. Salazar was a great lover of *son jarocho*.

In Mexican American music clubs throughout the US Southwest during the 1960s, rock 'n' roll bands often inspired by the Sir Douglas Quintet, who had a hit with "She's About a Mover," were emulated. A kind of Tex-Mex music became popular. But due to the Chicano power movement, dance halls started booking acts with such folkloric instruments as guitarrón, vihuela, jarana, and charango. Just as the Rolling Stones swooned about Delta bluesmen like Robert Johnson and John Lee Hooker, Chicano leaders embraced Mexican *ranchero* singers like Lola Beltrán and Amalia Mendoza. When Los Lobos released *La Pistola y el Corazón* in 1989, winning a Grammy Award, *son jarocho* regional Mexican music found an audience in North America.

Accordionist David Hidalgo, a member of Los Lobos, explained how his band helped popularize the redemptive power of *son jarocho* for Chicanos. "The thing was…after we broke the ice and people decided that they could accept what we were doing, everybody was longing for what we were doing," Hidalgo recalled. "Everybody had that need in them that hadn't been fulfilled or something. But we were playing this music that people said, 'Oh yeah, that's what I grew up with,' and so it started to click. Like the first gig we played in Florence, California, at the American Legion, it was a *tamalada* and we only knew about five songs, and we kept playing them over and over again. That was the first time that we played somewhere where there was old folks, there was kids dancing, there was teenagers, everybody was partying together. But we got all these folks up and everybody was dancing. It was like 'What is this?' I never had that feeling before."

II

Before collaborating with O'Farrill and Sehgal on this project, I knew little about the intense *communal* feeling that *fandangos* produce in Mexico. The style of dancing found at these events was foreign to me. But I was involved with US-Mexico immigration issues. Recently, I delivered the commencement address at St. Edward's University, a Catholic liberal arts school in Austin, Texas. Since 1972 the university has been the national leader in migrant education. Their College Assistance Migrant Program (CAMP) has offered access and opportunity for over 2,800 sons and daughters of migrant and seasonal farm workers. They are earning college diplomas courtesy of CAMP generosity. There is palpable pride at St. Edward's that Cesar Chavez had stayed on campus in 1966 to petition the Texas State legislature on better working conditions for farm workers in the Rio Grande Valley. "If the Department of Education ever pulled its money [from CAMP] we'd find ways to keep it going," George E. Martin, the president of St. Edward's, claims. "One of the great benefits we get out of this is it brings people together from all different backgrounds to educate each other about the subcultures and cultures that make up our community. You cannot truly educate someone without creating that cultural sensitivity."

One of the St. Edward's students who recently graduated was senior Jaqueline Olvera, whose passion is to help poor people through a combination of psychology and music. "Music has been a big part of my life," Jacqueline said. "I would like to become a counselor for individuals who could benefit from music therapy. Music has provided me with therapeutic benefits and I would like to share this with others."

For my commencement address I told the backstory of itinerant folksinger Woody Guthrie's song "Deportee." Guthrie was from rural Oklahoma but spent much of the Great Depression living in the Texas Panhandle, trying to survive the ecological destruction of the Dust Bowl. Today he is best known for writing the popular 1940 anthem "This Land is Your Land." But Woody, a prolific songwriter, also wrote "Deportee," a poignant protest ballad, about American arrogance and disregard toward Mexicans. In the age of Donald Trump's deriding Mexicans as "rapists," while simultaneously asking Congress to appropriate $21.6 billion (a conservative Department of Homeland Security estimate) to construct an imposing eighteen-foot-high border wall, Guthrie's seventy-year-old "Deportee" lament resonates mightily. "For millions of immigrants, both legal and undocumented, the virtual wall looms over their lives as the Berlin Wall did for East Germans," Hector Tobar recently wrote in the *New York Times.* "It's the work of an arbitrary and cruel political system that accepts the products of their labor while keeping them trapped in legal limbo."

Guthrie, an oracle for the down-and-out, was in New York City on January 29, 1948, when he read a tragic newspaper story about a US Immigration Services airplane crashing in Los Gatos, California. Thirty-two people died (four Americans and twenty-eight "braceros" farm workers). Even though he was a long three thousand miles away from the smoking debris near Coalinga, California, he privately mourned the lives wasted. And his humanitarian ire was raised because the four white Americans killed in the Los Gatos crash—pilot Francis Atkinson, flight attendant Bobbie Atkinson, copilot Marion Ewing, and immigration guard Frank Chaffin—were mentioned in the *New York Times* story, while the Mexican immigrants killed, by contrast, were lumped together as merely nameless "deportees." To the media of the early Cold War era, they were just throwaway agricultural fruit-pickers not deemed worthy of memorialization. Guthrie responded to this unconscionable reportorial omission by writing the lyrics to "Deportee," attaching symbolic names to the Mexican dead of the crash:

> *Goodbye to my Juan, goodbye, Rosalita,*
> *Adios mis amigos, Jesus y Maria;*
> *You won't have a name when you ride the big airplane,*
> *All they will call you will be "deportees"…*
> *Some of us are illegal, and some are not wanted,*
> *Our work contracts out and we have to move on;*
> *Six hundred miles to that Mexican border,*
> *They chase us like outlaws, like rustlers, like thieves…*
> *The sky plane caught on fire over Los Gatos Canyon,*

A fireball of lightning, and shook all our hills,
Who are these friends, all scattered like leaves?
The radio says, "They are just deportees"

During the 1980s, as a graduate student in US history at Georgetown University, I sang Guthrie's "Deportee" on guitar at blue-smoke coffeehouses and European street corners; it was a mainstay of my pass-the-basket repertoire. Guthrie's elegy about the deaths of Mexican migrant workers had a powerful and lasting effect on me. With imaginative hubris I even wrote my own last verse to Guthrie's song centered on how the Holy Cross brothers buried the nameless "deportees" in a Fresno, California, cemetery (mass grave).

Shovels were lifted, to dig a mass grave
No rosary was counted
No eulogy gave
Callin' familia would have cost 'em a fee
And all those burned bodies were just deportees.

My infatuation with all things Guthrie eventually led me to study the US-Mexican border ballads collected in the 1930s and 1940s by John and Ruby Lomax (and sometimes John's son, Alan). To earn a PhD at Georgetown you had to be conversant in two languages— Spanish became my strongest suit. Learning to sing the Latino *corridos* while playing my Gibson guitar helped me both lurch toward proficiency in Spanish and ponder the rich intercultural relations between the US and Mexico.

The US-Mexico border region extends from the Pacific Ocean (west) to the Gulf of Mexico (east). Novelist William S. Burroughs considered it an "interzone," where the sweaty atmosphere is jagged with history, betrayal, conflict, strife, redemption, and aspiration. Only Latin American magical realists like Gabriel García Márquez or Carlos Fuentes have ever adequately captured in prose the mind-bending surrealism of this interzone land of exchanges. On some afternoons the entire US-Mexican border feels like a giant waiting tank, a sort of purgatory between heaven and hell. The American side has the benefits of better engineering, sanitation, and public safety. Yet on the Mexican side joy and music and mysticism hold sway.

At present there are nearly fifty US-Mexico border crossing areas and over 300 binational ports of entry. Most of the security spots run with relative ease. Unfortunately, the media focuses attention on the drugs, cartels, and gangs along the border. What gets overlooked is the wonderful fact that citizens of border towns (both sides) are often bilingual, a great heads-up in the multicultural twenty-first century. And the musical styles and traditions of both the US and Mexico seamlessly blend together in an ethereal way along the borderlands. It's almost impossible to differentiate the ancient mores of, say, Brownsville or Matamoros. They are, in some cultural way, wired to the same vibrations. On any given afternoon in either city you can boogie to *rock en español* (Spanish twist to rock 'n' roll), *sonidero* (deejay mixing myriad musical genres), *tejano* (Tex-Mex style), and *technobanda* (based on village brass bands). However, it's the border *corridos*, the musical crossroads where history meets mythmaking, that speaks most authoritatively to the struggles of past decades.

Border *corridos* were first popularized circa 1848, after the US won the Mexican-American War. According to the Texas State Historical Society, most *corridos* following "Mr. Polk's War" were eight-syllable ballads, with four-line stanzas in major keys sung to celebrate Mexican history. They were traditionally performed in quick-paced waltz time. Today musicologists compare them to having an almost polka pulse. In some parts of Mexico, *corridos* are sung by balladeers at festivals and in public spaces, often lamenting lost love. The *despedidas* (farewell) that close these *corridos* are heartbreaking. Spanish-written lines like *Ya con esta me despido* ("With this I take my leave") or *Vuela, vuela, palomita* ("Fly, fly, little dove") eventually lured most listeners into a melancholic state.

One particularly sorrowful romantic *corrido* that has currency in modern times, even recorded by Bob Dylan in 1974, is "Spanish Is the Loving Tongue." Back in 1915, coinciding with World War I, the Western American poet Charles Badger Clark wrote this *corrido* under the title "A Border Affair." It's the saga of a love-crossed relationship between a sweet Mexican woman and a rough-and-tumble American cowboy. The premise of Clark's song is that border authorities banned this particular in-love cowboy from returning to Mexico because of an unpaid gambling debt. Every line is fraught with emotional weight, ending with "Never seen her since that night, I can't cross the Line, you know."

It's the protest-infused type of *corrido*, however, that came to musical fruition in late nineteenth-century US-Mexico border towns that resonates in our current Age of Trump. Border *corridos*, the fulminating against oppression in song, often portrayed Mexican day-laborers living along the Rio Grande River as earnest revolutionaries and freedom fighters rallying against overt US military power and racial oppression. Perhaps the most historically significant of these was "El Corrido de Gregorio Cortez." I first learned about this Mexican outlaw from reading Professor Americo Paredes's fine book *With His Pistol in His Hand* (1958), long ago, while in graduate school at Georgetown. The saga of Gregorio Cortez seemed to me, then, as now, like a Billy the Kid outlaw tall tale, only with the outcast being of Mexican ancestry.

The drama for this popular *corrido* begins on June 12, 1901, at the Thulemeyer Ranch in Karnes County, Texas. Day laborer Gregorio Cortez and his brother Romaldo worked as cow-hands for this prosperous Anglo Texas family. From sunup to sundown they toiled on the ranch. But, that June afternoon, Sheriff W. T. Morris and his deputies John Trimmell and Boone Choate arrived unannounced on the Thulmeyer property, waving badges, pronouncing that they were tracking down a Mexican horse thief. Choate began interrogating the Cortez brothers, who spoke only broken English. This created a linguistic gulf, which soon proved fatal. When Choate asked Gregorio if he had *traded* a horse, he said, "No." The deputy didn't comprehend that, in Mexican culture, there is a *vast* difference between a horse (*caballo*) and a mare (*yegua*). So Cortez had answered truthfully—a mare had been swapped, *not* a horse.

On the spot the sheriff accused Gregorio Cortez of being a congenital liar. He deemed him guilty of the high crime of horse thievery. When the deputies tried to arrest the brothers Gregorio balked, defiantly telling the Texas authorities, "*No me puede arrestar por nada*" (you cannot arrest me for anything). Boone Choate, who was serving as interpreter, asserted that Gregorio had proclaimed "No white man can arrest me." A skirmish ensued. Falsely assuming that the Cortez brothers were unarmed, Sheriff Morris drew his pistol. Romaldo, seeking to protect his brother, tried to knock the weapon away from the sheriff. Instead he was shot (not fatal). Then the sheriff fired at Gregorio, missing his head by a whisker. Cortez pulled out a pistol from under his shirt and killed Morris with perfect bull's-eye aim. Recognizing his life was in the balance, Gregorio darted off, lickety-split, disappearing into the thick scrub brush and mesquite thickets. Like from a scene in a Wild West movie, the deputies chased Gregorio, suddenly a desperado, while the sheriff alerted the Texas Rangers stationed in San Antonio to join the manhunt. Gregorio, however, evaded his pursuers, disappearing into the desert wilderness and somehow evading the bloodhounds.

An all-points bulletin was issued by the Texas police for the apprehension of Gregorio Cortez. Bounties were posted for his arrest across south Texas. A posse of three hundred men, including a contingent of Texas Rangers, went on a " Wanted: Dead or Alive" chase. Avoiding apprehension by the *rinches* (Mexican name for rangers) for days, full of survivalist cunning, the legend of Gregorio Cortez was born in Hispanic Texas and Mexican border towns. Eluding capture, Cortez traversed over a hundred miles and horse-backed around four hundred miles across the desolate plains. Eventually, however, Jesús "El Teco" González, who would get portrayed in the *corrido* as a Judas-like figure, squealed to the Texas Rangers about Gregorio's whereabouts. He was holed up at Absánde la Garza's sheep shack in Cotulla. Surrounded by the heavily armed posse, Cortez blasted away in a blaze of bullets, killing another sheriff. Eventually, Cortez, terribly outnumbered, surrendered. He was jailed in San Antonio and awaited trial.

The Hispanic community of south Texas, especially along the border and in San Antonio, embraced Cortez as a symbolic underdog hero. By standing tall against systemic racism and police brutality he became a martyr. Fear was widespread that Gregorio would be lynched. Mexican border community Catholic churches said prayers for him. A few wealthy Mexican Americans living in Texas even established a legal defense fund for Cortez. Eventually he made it to trial and was found guilty of murder and sentenced to life in prison at the Texas State Penitentiary at Huntsville. Improvisational poems were sung by *guitarreros* all over Old Mexico praising his bravery.

In a strange twist of fate, Cortez procured an early release from the Huntsville prison when he was proven innocent of horse theft. His martyrdom skyrocketed even more. His release coincided with the ongoing Mexican Revolution, started three years prior, in 1910. He was now embraced as a Mexican American cultural hero, and new verses of the "El corrido de Gregorio Cortez" were added by folk musicians all along the US-Mexican border.

I thought of Gregorio Cortez recently when I toured the Alamo in San Antonio, considered the "shrine to Texas freedom," to offer historical commentary for a documentary film on the Texas Revolution of 1836. Because the public history presentation at the Alamo is one-sided, essentially portraying only the heroism of the US citizens like Davy Crockett of Tennessee, William Travis of South Carolina, and James Bowie of Kentucky, I also thought about Guthrie's "Deportee." A significant segment of the three million annual tourists that travel to the fabled Alamo complain that the weathered limestone structures are smaller and less impressive than expected. A common refrain heard on the Spanish-style plaza in front is "That's it?"

This initial first reaction to the Alamo is unfortunate. For, in my opinion, the old Spanish mission and frontier covenant are the ideal place to contemplate the long, fraught relationship between the US and Mexico. The problem isn't in the smallness of the edifices but in the lopsided way the history is spun. The hundreds of Mexicans who died in the San Antonio battle aren't given proper historical due at the Alamo Museum. The dead Mexican soldiers are lumped together without their gallant stories of heroism properly revealed. And the brave Tejanos who died defending the Alamo alongside Crockett, Travis, and Bowie—men with Mexican names like Juan Abamillo, Carlos Espalier, Juan A. Badillo, Gregorio Esparza, Antonio Fuentes, and Adrés Nava—are given short shrift.

As Kabir Sehgal points out in this book, when the Texas Revolution of 1836 began, Anglo Americans held a 5 to 1 ratio over Mexicans. Hoping to reverse the trend, Mexican President General Antonio López de Santa Anna—nicknamed the Napoleon of the West—ordered the eviction of "illegal settlers" in Texas. The situation soon turned combustible and strains US and Mexico relations to this very day. Stephen Austin, famously defiant, wrote a letter urging Anglo Texans to disregard all orders from Santa Anna. The Mexican Congress then voted that the Mexican government could legally kill any male insurrectionists. Sam Houston and other Texas leaders sought the Lone Star Republic, breaking away from Mexico. This led to the clash at the Alamo—a thirteen-day siege from February 23 to March 6, 1836, which Santa Anna actually won. But forty-six days later, at the Battle of San Jacinto, near modern-day Houston, the Texans defeated the Mexican army of Santa Anna.

Once Texas won its independence in 1836, the Hispanic population was immediately disenfranchised. Before long political representation vanished entirely, for decades. Only slowly, in the twentieth century due to the 1960s Chicano rights movement, did Hispanics regain some of the political power in the Texas, California, Arizona, and New Mexico state legislatures.

Wandering around the Alamo's compound, I was reminded about how quarrelsome US-Mexican relations have been for so long. Part of the problem is purposeful history amnesia and distortion of facts. Things had deteriorated mightily in recent decades. The demonization of Spanish-speaking people in America has reared boondoggles of the most dehumanizing kind like the George W. Bush administration's erecting a border barrier. President Trump now is determined to make the border wall even bigger and longer. It's so sad that the US-Mexico border—so rich in culture and biodiversity—is stuck in a toxic climate of violence and mistrust. The idea of Trump's border wall is just the latest insult to Mexican identity: a variation on the *New York Times* omission of Mexicans of the Los Gatos crash of 1948 and the discounting of Mexican and Tejano heroes of the 1836 Battle of the Alamo.

III

I think of this multimedia project—book, album, and film documentary—as correctives to one-sided history, educational in nature, the balancing of the scale against an onslaught of Trumpian screeds and distortions. *Folklórico* groups (dance troupes) and Afro Latin jazz musicians pouring their hearts out performing "El Cascabel" is far more soulful than the president of the US deriding Haiti as a "shithole" country. Who doesn't agree that *fandango* ensembles are preferable to rogue US politicians spewing hate?

So O'Farrill and Sehgal swung into rhythmic and harmonic action after meeting Jorge Castillo, founder of Fandango Fronterizo. Born in El Paso, Texas, but currently living in Tijuana, Castillo is a retired librarian who teaches *son jarocho* workshops to children and adults. Since 2008, on every last Saturday in May, the fifty-eight-year-old Castillo organizes a jam session consisting of the *arpa, jarana,* and *requinto jarocho* to play at the border wall in Tijuana. "I learned to play guitar when I was a kid. Later in life, I fell in love with *fandangos.* To me they were an eye-opening event. It was love at first sight." Together Castillo, O'Farrill, and Sehgal decided to record an album right after the Fandango Fronterizo festival on May 26, 2018, in Playas de Tijuana with the wall that divided Tijuana and San Diego as the backdrop. Their vision was to mix an ensemble of *son jarochos* musicians with traditional folk singers, improvisational poets, fandango dancers, modern jazz artists, and passersby yelling "*Otra! Otra!*" Young people learning about Mexican folkloric traditions treated the afternoons like educational seminars. They realize there is more to Mexican music than "La Bamba," and that walls can't stop the free flow of sound. "Art is ahead of its time," Sehgal says. "Just as there is a Monroe Doctrine, there is also a Fandango Doctrine, which states that music and art transcend politics in the Western Hemisphere."

Rehearsal for *Fandango at the Wall* took place at the Casa de la Cultura patio in Playas de Tijuana. I was amazed at how well the Tijuana Youth Chorus (aged nine to seventeen) were able to learn O'Farrill's quite complicated jazz compositions. If there is such a thing as free-form Afro-Caribbean-Mexican jazz, then this orchestra was the all-star musical exemplar. The convergence of mixing three-hundred-year-old Iberian music with modern-day post–free jazz rhythms was phenomenal.

Fandango Fronterizo was a glorious occasion for both San Diego and Playas de Tijuana. With the blue Pacific Ocean shared by both nations, only an artificial steel-pillar wall separates the twin cities. Because the wall is not concrete, light shines through the bars. There was an abiding sense that Memorial Day weekend that the ocean and air were borderless in beauty. On the Mexican side, where I stood, there was a marble memorial commemorating the ending of the Mexican-American War (established by a joint commission). Right next to it a tarima (wood block) served as stage for the days of dancing. Playas de Tijuana *fandango* began with the *zapateado* dancing and musicians strumming melodies on a sea of guitars. Players appeared from all points to hold a musical ritual at the wall. Nearby food vendors sold everything from churros to shrimp tacos to tamales. Bright flowers in communal gardens abounded. Many of the Veracruz musicians present had made their own instruments, which they played with subtlety and all manner of excellence. The power of strings and violins resonated through the wall from both sides. Dogs barked. Seagulls scoured for bread crumbs. Cheers of "Epa!" were shouted. Children laughed at the grand cacophony of sound, the blending of styles and cultures, the sway of the crowd. The entire afternoon glowed of ritual music transported from the Atlantic Seaboard of Veracruz to the sandy Pacific beach of our dreams.

The irresistible Villalobos Brothers, especially, stole my heart away in the powerful bright sunshine. Two of the brothers—Luis and Alberto—played accomplished violin on the Mexican side of the wall. The third brother, Ernesto, masterfully played his violin on the US side. The message was obvious: Music knows no walls.

As part of O'Farrill's no-walls philosophy, his orchestra included musicians from all parts of the world. Oudist Rahim AlHaj of Iraq and tarist Sahba Motallebi of Iran were included in the musical revue. The great violinist Regina Carter—MacArthur Genius Grant recipient—was there to bring a timeless soul into the public dance. Drum virtuoso Antonio Sanchez of Mexico City gave the performance a hypnotic edge that provoked attention and admiration. Friends, family, and community gathered on both sides of the border wall to play with each other and interact across the wall. Then, on June 4 and 5 in New York, at the Power Station studio, the album was finished with even more guest artists lending their talents such as Mandy Gonzalez, who has Mexican heritage and stars in the Broadway hit *Hamilton*. O'Farrill and Sehgal's idea to give *son jarocho* music its day in the sun was influenced by the success of guitarist Ry Cooder and Cuban bandleader Juan de Marcos Gonzáles's *The Buena Vista Social Club*. Back in 1996 Cooder and Gonzales conceived of *The Buena Vista Social Club* as a long-overdue celebration of Cuban music. Hoping to let jazz music bring the Cuban and American people together, their effort earned them the rank of number 260 on *Rolling Stone* magazine's list of 500 greatest albums *ever*. The recording sessions grew in stature because German filmmaker Wim Wenders did a tremendous job on the documentary that accompanied the project. Opening with "Chan Chan," the group's signature song, the fourteen-track album, which won a Grammy Award for Best Traditional Tropical Latin Album in 1990, featured such amazing Cuban musicians as bassist Orlando Cachaito López and guitarist Eliades Ochoa. Most of the songs on the album, recorded in Havana, comprised standards of the nueva trova and filin repertoire. The song "Candela," with lyrics sizzling with lovemaking, is considered a classic *son jarocho* composition.

Fandango at the Wall casts these *son jarocho* musicians as the veritable stars: Patricio Hidalgo, Ramón Gutiérrez, Tacho Utrera, Fernando Guadarrama, Wendy Cao, Martha Vega Hernandez, Zenen Zeferino, and Jorge Castillo, among others. These are tried-and-true practitioners of the craft. There are many contenders for the "Chan Chan" of this production, from "El Siquisiri," which starts every *fandango*, to Hidalgo's "Conga Patria," which seems to make everyone dance.

Yet there are clear differences between the approaches of *Fandango at the Wall* and *Buena Vista Social Club*. While O'Farrill and Sehgal were most concerned with the human tragedy of the US-Mexico border wall, their ecological consciousness is also part of the *Fandango* project. What concerns them most is a chain of US Fish and Wildlife (FW) refuges in the lower Rio Grande Valley in Texas. This area, home to numerous endangered species like the ocelot (beautiful wildcats with spotted leopard-like coats of fur) would be ecologically devastated if a man-made barrier is erected. Anti-wall activists have protested that a barrier dividing the two countries would disrupt the small wild cat's migration routes. Biologists are trying to protect and restore wildlife corridors for the ocelots along the US-Mexican border, but Trump's wall would destroy the habitat necessary for the mammal, one of the most exquisite creatures on the planet, to survive. The border would cause "serious, and likely irreparable wildlife and habitat loss and damage," as one US Fish and Wildlife leader put it, unraveling decades of conservation initiatives to rehabilitate the Lower Rio Grande Valley National Wildlife areas. Wildlife corridors between the US and Mexico are needed instead of a wall that would cause extinction of flora and fauna. And in the US, over two-thirds of the border is owned by various banks, ranchers, tribes, state governments, and private parties. In order for Trump's huge wall to truly happen, a blizzard of legal tangles would have to be overcome.

History will show Trump's border wall as a desperate last-gasp effort to keep America Caucasian while Fandango Fronterizo points to the multicultural future. The president's refusal to denounce neo-Nazis in Charlottesville, Virginia, in August 2017 will go down as a low-ebb moment in the annals of US presidential history. "My grandmother used to say—'*Digame con quien caminas, y te dire quien eres*'—Tell me who you walk with, and I'll tell you who you are," said Rep. Adriano Espaillat (D-New York), who represents most of Harlem and is an immigrant from the Dominican Republic. "If he's walking around with white supremacists and supporting them, this kind of talk doesn't surprise me."

When campaigning to become president of Mexico in the spring of 2018, Andrés Manuel López Obrador—from a podium just across the Rio Grande from El Paso—ably expressed the wrath of millions of Mexicans who feel belittled by Trump's cruel taunts. "No threat, no wall, no bullying attitude from some foreign government," he said, "is going to keep us from being better and happy in our own country."

O'Farrill and Sehgal and the rest of the *Fandango* team planted a flag of peace and friendship between Mexico and the US with the joyous festival, live concert, album, and this book. The resistance to Trump's monstrous wall, in the end, won't succeed. Activists like Sehgal and O'Farrill are opening hearts, one at a time, with the uplift of unrestrained melodies. As Plato knew, art and music can revolutionize the world one beat at a time.

One evening in Playas de Tijuana, I walked along the border wall that runs straight into the Pacific Ocean with O'Farrill and Sehgal. The sun was setting and the lull of the surf was meditative. Sayings like "Love Trumps Wall" and "Earth Was Not Meant to Have Walls" were painted on the fence pilings. A verse from Woody Guthrie's "This Land Is Your Land," the timeless populist ballad that unites the disenfranchised and downtrodden, danced in my head. It stands, in a sense, as the enduring inspiration for the entire *Fandango at the Wall* project:

> *As I went walking I saw a sign there.*
> *And on the sign it said "No trespassing."*
> *But on the other side, it didn't say nothing.*
> *That side was made for you and me.*

Or as Arturo O'Farrill and Kabir Sehgal say, "No more walls."

Douglas Brinkley
Playas de Tijuana, Mexico,
and San Diego, California, USA
May 24–27, 2018

Arturo O'Farrill and Jorge Castillo hug after performing at the border wall in May 2018

Arturo O'Farrill and Rahim AlHaj shaking hands

INTRODUCTION

"Poor Mexico! So far from God and so
close to the United States."[1]
—PORFIRIO DÍAZ, president of Mexico and general

"Everyone will remember me being who I am,
what I was and what I will be."[2]
—MARÍA FÉLIX, Mexican singer and actress

"Our two countries owe their independence to the fact
that your ancestors and mine held the same truths to be
worth fighting for and dying for. Hidalgo and Juarez were
men of the same stamp as Washington and Jefferson."[3]
—FRANKLIN D. ROOSEVELT,
32nd president of the United States

As you travel through Mexico, from the coastal beaches of Tijuana to the rustic villages of Veracruz, you'll eventually come across a familiar saying: *al mal tiempo, buena cara*, which means to put on a brave face in spite of a tough situation. Or put another way, grin and bear it. This phrase speaks to the challenges of living in a developing country where life isn't always easy, yet the people demonstrate a resolute grit to make the most out of any situation.

In recent years, Mexico's political leaders have had to internalize this phrase with respect to the US. In 2017, some 65 percent of Mexicans held a negative view of the US, up from 29 percent in 2015.[4]

It isn't so easy to look the other way, especially as the invectives and insults toward Mexico have continued unabated.

The verbal slaps began as soon as Donald Trump descended by escalator into the lobby of the Trump Tower on June 16, 2015, to announce his candidacy for the Republican nomination for president. Before he declared his intention to run, he established the premise of his campaign: America was losing, and others were taking advantage of it. He cited Japan, China, and ISIS as offenders, but saved his most pointed remarks when describing our neighbor to the south:

> When do we beat Mexico at the border? They're laughing at us, at our stupidity. And now they are beating us economically. They are not our friend, believe me. But they're killing us economically…When Mexico sends its people, they're not sending their best. They're not sending you. They're not sending you. They're sending people that have lots of problems, and they're bringing those problems with us. They're bringing drugs. They're bringing crime. They're rapists. And some, I assume, are good people.[5]

At the time, his comments were chalked up as the utterances of a celebrity dilettante whose opinion didn't matter. But with history as our guide, the speech will go down as the politically shrewd opening salvo of the most unlikely person ever to win the presidency. Trump's fiercely nationalist remarks heralded an unapologetic populism arguably not seen since President Andrew Jackson, who served in the nineteenth century and engaged in class warfare to win over the support of the common people. Whereas Jackson railed against the ruling elites as corrupt and contemptible, Trump aimed his ire at another group of people: Mexicans. And if it wasn't clear who was responsible for the problems ailing America, he culminated his speech in no uncertain terms:

> I would build a great wall, and nobody builds walls better than me, believe me, and I'll build them very inexpensively, I will build a great, great wall on our southern border. And I will have Mexico pay for that wall. Mark my words.[6]

Translation: Mexicans are responsible for our problems, and I will keep them out. You might expect the Republican nominee to advance a more tried-and-true message of self-reliance, that we are responsible for our own problems. But then again, the far right has long considered undocumented Mexicans as trespassers and transgressors, and President Trump is just the latest and most conspicuous conservative to advance this argument. His call to "build a wall" isn't a terribly new notion, as it's circulated among Republican circles for decades.

"I'll build that security fence, and we'll close it, and we'll say, 'Listen Jose, you're not coming in this time!'" exclaimed Pat Buchanan when he ran for the Republican nomination for the presidency in 1996.[7] But Trump's ascendancy has raised the specter of implementing this idea, and by extension, awakened a deep sense of fear, suspicion, and anxiety among the American people that the "illegals" are coming for their jobs.

Their fear is misplaced. But their questions aren't. Moreover, Trump isn't wrong in raising immigration as an issue worthy of debate. He is right that hundreds of thousands of jobs in the US auto sector have been lost, in the decades since the North American Free Trade Agreement (NAFTA) was implemented. At the same time, Mexico has lost millions of jobs in agriculture as their products compete against subsidized US farm goods. Yet in the years to come, American and Mexican workers might have more to dread from the wave of automation that will reshape the labor force as we know it.

Nor is Trump incorrect in wanting America to have safe and secure borders: A primary responsibility of the government is to protect its people and sovereignty. He's right that drugs flow in from the southern border, just as money and guns flow north to south. With undocumented immigrants comes a litany of social, economic, political, and security concerns that are wholly legitimate to debate, discuss, and decide upon.

But Trump has decided that undocumented Mexicans are violent criminals. He wrongly connects immigration with crime, when research suggests that they are inversely correlated.[8] Though he tried to caveat his remarks with "some…are good people," he hasn't walked back or apologized for his sweeping generalizations and falsifications. Since the beginning of his presidency through mid-2018, he had made 71 untrue statements that mention Mexico, and 327 that were about immigration, according to the *Washington Post*.[9] Even after then-candidate Trump traveled to Mexico to meet with its president in August 2016, he didn't relent from his assertions that undocumented Mexicans were trouble. When was the last time you heard him heralding the benefits of having a close relationship with Mexico?

Even though Trump hasn't succeeded yet in building a wall, he has arguably created one in the minds of Americans. This is a border born of distrust, discomfort, and distress, in which Americans may start to dam themselves off not just from Mexicans, but from those who are from elsewhere. As *Time* magazine puts it, "Walls have always been, at the most basic level, a form of communication" that send the message "stay away."[10] Trump's "build a wall" mantra is metastasizing from bumper sticker to executive order, while other more nuanced proposals that could strengthen the US-Mexico relationship are overlooked.

Fandango at the Wall presents an alternative vision of cross-border relations, one conceived by mutual appreciation and artistry. It gives Americans a new narrative in understanding our relationship with Mexico. It doesn't advocate for open borders but open hearts. We use prose to explore the historical relationship between the two countries, lyrics to expand empathy regarding what it means to be an immigrant in America, and music to raise awareness that Mexicans and Americans have more in common than just a border but also families, friends, and futures.

Fandango at the Wall is inspired by Jorge Francisco Castillo, a librarian in Chula Vista, California, who started the Fandango Fronterizo festival in 2008. He was working as a volunteer while cleaning up Tijuana beaches when he saw the border wall between the US and Mexico. He thought it would be a terrific location for a *fandango*, a festival in which musicians and members of the public gather. Every year since then, he and his fellow organizers have held the festival in the spring, in which participants make music on both sides of the border

Jorge Francisco Castillo at home in Tijuana

wall between San Diego and Tijuana. They perform a *fandango* that features *son jarocho* music from the Mexican coastal state of Veracruz. This music usually has only two chords, so anyone can sing, strum, or dance along. The constant vamping can easily put you into a meditative trance—not typically the feeling that the border wall evokes. The music travels through the mesh, and the festival becomes an incredible experience of coming-together of families and friends.

Acclaimed jazz musician and my frequent collaborator Arturo O'Farrill came across a story about Jorge in *The New York Times* in 2016. We discussed whether the Fandango Fronterizo could be grist for a new work. I traveled to Tijuana to meet with Jorge in May 2017, and we agreed to embark upon this creative journey together. From May 24 to May 27, 2018, Arturo and I led a delegation, in which we brought over thirty musicians to the San Diego–Tijuana wall to per-

6

form and record an album that would blur three borders: (1) physical borders with musicians on different sides of the border; (2) musical borders with artists from various genres; and (3) recording borders by capturing the music in live and studio environments.

We accomplished the first goal by recording musicians in both the US and Mexico. As for realizing the second objective, we wanted to feature iconic *son jarocho* musicians. Jorge helped us identify and bring Patricio Hidalgo, Ramón Gutiérrez, Tacho Utrera, Fernando Guadarrama, Wendy Cao, and Martha Vega Hernandez, among others, from Veracruz. In addition, we brought the eighteen-piece Afro Latin Jazz Orchestra from New York. We broadened the genres on the project by bringing and featuring several notable guest artists such as Regina Carter, a MacArthur "Genius" Fellow; Antonio Sanchez, a Mexican-American Golden Globe nominee and multi-Grammy winner who scored the music to *Birdman*; Rahim alHaj (and his trio), an acclaimed oud player from Iraq; Sahba Motallebi, a talented tar player from Iran; Akua Dixon, a gifted cellist; the Villalobos Brothers (Ernesto, Luis, and Alberto), three brothers who play the violin, originally from Veracruz and now based in the US; and Jose "Gurri" Gurria-Cardenas, an imaginative composer and percussionist from Mexico.

We achieved the third goal by recording live performances at the Tijuana border wall and at the Casa de la Cultura in Playas de Tijuana (a cultural center in Tijuana). We also recorded the actual Fandango Fronterizo festival in which there are musicians on both sides of the border wall. For example, two of the Villalobos brothers were in Tijuana, and the other was in San Diego. We finished the recording in the Power Station studio in New York City from June

4 to June 6, 2018. It was there where more guest artists joined us such as Grammy-nominated rapper Ana Tijoux, who is a frequent visitor of the Fandango Fronterizo; and Mandy Gonzalez, who has Mexican heritage and stars in Broadway's *Hamilton*. Jorge and a few New York–based *son jarocho* musicians also collaborated with us, such as Zenen Zeferino, Claudia Montes, and Julia del Palacio. After each session, I would hustle home to finish this manuscript.

This Book

The goal of this book is to put our music-making experience in broader context. First, I document the efforts involved in the recording project, in the chapter "Fandango for the Future," which seeks to repair the rift between the US and Mexico by creating a new foundation of understanding based on the arts. Admittedly, this chapter could serve as liner notes for the record, and I wanted to share the "behind the scenes" of the music, to give you a better idea of how people from various cultures came together for this production. This first chapter replaces the "build a wall" mantra with an invitation to "join me at the *fandango*," a communal Mexican festival. Healing the wounds between the US and Mexico can be done on a person-by-person basis, by putting a face on each culture, and treating others with respect and dignity. When government officials are at loggerheads, artists and private citizens must step in and up. And that's really the takeaway from our project—everyone can play a role in bringing our countries and people together.

And what better way to bring folks together than music? Some of the songs were inspired not just by the people and traditions of the borderlands, but the natural habitat of these parts. For example,

"Jaiicasosebaim Noone" is a piece inspired by the indigenous people of the Sonora region. "Hummingbird Blues" is about these colorful creatures in the region. Often omitted in the debate over building the border wall is its effects on the environment. Chapter two, "Requiem for the Borderlands," notes the indigenous wildlife and vegetation of this stunning terrain, and how these living creatures, from pygmy owls to jaguars, would be negatively affected when concrete and crushed rock are introduced.

Of course, I don't believe in open borders and I realize that the history between the US and Mexico is long and complicated. And I wanted to chronicle some of the ups and downs of our past, and to place our project into a fuller context. Thus, the third chapter, "Brick by Brick," is a brief history of how the US-Mexico border came to be,

Rahim AlHaj (left), Sourena Sefati (center), Sahba Motallebi (right)

from armed conflicts to negotiated purchases. Initially the border was a frontier policed by vigilantes and eventually hardened into a divide of steel and barbed wire with drones watching from the skies.

Given an understanding of US-Mexico history, one might consider the current diplomatic row between our two countries as not a reason for despair or worry. But let's not accept such dismissiveness or complacency. Because left unchecked, these forces can manifest into darker rhetoric and even hateful actions. Chapter four, "The Mental Dam," is a short study of the recurring xenophobia that has gripped both the US and Mexico over two hundred years. Just as Americans have periodically implemented laws to inhibit Mexicans from migrating, so too have Mexicans resisted the *gringo* colonists from coming to their country. The US-Mexico relationship has been beset by everything from bans and boycotts to lies and lynch mobs—and undocumented children separated from their families.

After beginning with a forceful call for the arts, the book ends with an unvarnished look at the truth. The final chapter, "The Walls Came Tumbling Down," is about setting the record straight and sharing the true nature of US-Mexico relations, from how many Mexican nationals come to America to their impact on our economy and society. The facts show how the US and Mexico are closely intertwined, from finances to families. It distinguishes between "Mexicans" who are obviously from Mexico and "Hispanics" who are people from Spanish-speaking countries in Latin America.

After reading the book, I hope you'll want to explore the other parts of the project, particularly the album and eventual film. Or if you want to start with the music before reading this text, I won't blame you!

The Formats

Fandango at the Wall is a three-part, interdisciplinary work that considers the past, present, and future of US-Mexico relations:

1. **Book**—This book puts the current diplomatic row between both nations in its historical context. It comes with a CD of eight songs: four *son jarocho* songs; two "Middle Eastern" sounding pieces by Rahim AlHaj Trio and Sahba Motallebi; and two pieces performed by Arturo O'Farrill and the Afro Latin Jazz Orchestra with special guests. These songs are just a sample of the full musical repertoire. You will find the lyrics and translations to all the *son jarocho* songs (which aren't all part of this book/CD but are found in the full musical offering sold and available separately) in the appendix of this book. The book is also available in digital and e-reader formats. There is an audio book version which features Douglas Brinkley reading the foreword and me reading the narrative and the afterword, which was written by Ambassador Andrew Young. Arturo O'Farrill performs a solo piano underscore during sections of my readings.

2. **Album**—The album serves as a model of what collaboration and cooperation among the US, Mexico, and countries all around the world can look and sound like. When people from different cultures come together, they can produce works of meaning, that hopefully entertain audiences and perhaps even provoke more introspection.

The complete music includes a repertoire of nearly thirty songs that we recorded as part of the live and studio sessions. These songs include all of the *son jarocho* songs and all the pieces performed by Arturo O'Farrill and the Afro Latin Jazz Orchestra featuring special guests. The music spans countries and cultures, borders and barriers. The music is sold separately, either as a digital download or a two-CD physical package. It's also available on streaming services.

3. **Film**—The documentary highlights the personal stories involved in the making of this project. It shows what life is like in Veracruz for the *son jarocho* musicians. It provides a glimpse into the lives of Jorge, who lives in Tijuana, and Arturo, who resides in Brooklyn. The film crew captured the rehearsals, performances, and plenty of "down time" in which the musicians were getting to know one another. This film initiative is still a work in progress. The cinematographer of our film won an Emmy Award for his work on *Cartel Land*, a documentary about vigilantes in the US and Mexico, and which also was nominated for an Academy Award for Best Documentary Feature. In our film *Fandango at the Wall*, the camera "moves" like another instrument as it encircles the musicians and dancers, while they perform. Our hope is that the film makes you feel like you're at a *fandango*.

No matter the format or medium, I hope the intent with which we created *Fandango at the Wall* shines through: to bring our countries and people together through music. Our project showcases *son jarocho* musicians and how their music can serve not only as the heartbeat of *fandango* but friendship across countries and cultures.

In exploring this work, perhaps more will be awakened to the shared heritage and humanity of those on both sides of the border. Ultimately, our project is one of convergence. In spite of the political climate, artists and activists aren't just waiting for a better tomorrow. We're trying to make today better, too.

And besides, I didn't want to just write a book with no solutions, or for that matter, make a banal call for "more education." Rather, all of those involved have humbly attempted to create an example of what partnership can be. Our music reflects what is in our hearts, and we produced a soundtrack for what US and Mexico relations may one day become. Art is prescient, and we hope that these melodies and harmonies can help us see through these walls and usher in an era of more mellow and harmonious relations.

Kabir Sehgal
Playas de Tijuana, Mexico
and San Diego, California USA
May 24–27, 2018

Performing at the border wall in Tijuana in May 2018

Arturo O'Farrill, the Afro Latin Jazz Orchestra, and special guests play at the border wall in Tijuana May 2018

14

Chapter 1

FANDANGO FOR THE FUTURE

How art builds bridges
between the US and Mexico

"Be it the edge of time or space,
there is nothing so awe-inspiring as a border."[1]
—YUKIO MISHIMA, Japanese author

"People say that *son jarocho* has not only African and Spanish roots
but indigenous roots as well. This enriches the perspective of unity,
even more, among different cultures. The fusion of cultures
originated a new musical expression."[2]
—AGUSTÍN DEL MORAL TEJEDA, Mexican author

"The only thing that can cross besides
the birds and the winds is the music."[3]
—JORGE CASTILLO, founder of Fandango Fronterizo

Before Jackie Robinson played his first Major League Baseball game in 1947 or the Voting Rights Act was enacted in 1965, black and white jazz musicians performed together in the 1920s. In a sense, these musicians embodied an ideal vision of a future without segregation and institutionalized racism. Their music evoked the "better angels" of the American people. You could say that "America the Beautiful" doesn't just refer to a song but reflects the spirit of the many musicians of various races, faiths, and backgrounds who were ahead of their times, and who tried to radiate respect, tolerance, and empathy. And maybe for these reasons, art can be unnerving. It provokes audiences to consider uncomfortable ideas and arrangements, which are showcased without hesitation. When something is more familiar, it becomes less frightening.

These days the political relationship between the US and Mexico is nothing if not uncomfortable, so several of us artists banded together to create a music recording that illustrates how we can listen to one another and work together across barriers and dividers. We were irritated and disappointed with the prevailing demonization of immigrants. And in short, we wanted to bring the people of our two nations together through music.

So we launched *Fandango at the Wall*, a three-part, interdisciplinary testament and tribute to the power of arts and culture. By exploring this content, we hope that more people will come away with a better understanding of specific cultural traditions, and also draw inspiration to find ways of working with others across differences and barriers of any kind.

We want this project to encourage more artists from both countries to participate in "jam session" diplomacy, in which they work together on fresh creative endeavors, so that audiences on both sides of the border can be exposed to new ideas, narratives, and traditions.

The US Department of State hired jazz bands to represent America abroad in the 1940s and 1950s. The Voice of America radio broadcast the sounds of Duke Ellington to the Soviet Union, as millions of listeners tuned into these dulcet and bluesy sounds. Following this tradition of leveraging music to win hearts and minds, perhaps current or former foreign policy officials can adopt a "*fandango* doctrine" in which they work with artists to stage more cross-border *fandangos*. I would like to see more artists and diplomats working together to advance harmony and goodwill across the US-Mexico border and beyond.

While there is a need for these types of collaborative projects, there isn't always the funding. That's why it's important for public and private institutions, as well as private citizens, to step into the void, so that artists can fill the gaps that exist between our two countries. Maybe the National Endowment for the Arts can prioritize programs that facilitate cultural exchange programs between the US and Mexico. Or Kickstarter and other crowd-funding websites can actively promote projects that span both counties. If you feel compelled to "do something" about the US-Mexico border dispute, not only can you call your senator, but you can look out for artists with whom you want to collaborate or support.

No matter the funding obstacles, artists are incredibly resourceful and are already working on cross-border art installations and various cultural exchange programs. Artists possess an indefatigable creative spirit that cannot be restrained or limited by barriers and walls.

Looking to play a small role in bringing our countries together, Arturo and I gravitated to what we know. And we quickly grew absorbed with the sounds of Southwestern Mexico. This music continues to reverberate within us. I'm listening to a playlist with this type of music as I write these words.

The Sound of Veracruz

You don't have to travel to Veracruz, a coastal state in Southeastern Mexico, to be familiar with its music, which is known as *son jarocho*. Perhaps the most famous *son jarocho* song in the US is "La Bamba." It was popularized by rock and roll artist Ritchie Valens in 1958 and later by Los Lobos in the 1980s. The tune swept the country and has remained a recognizable hit. I remember lip synching the song as a kid in the 1990s. But this piece is just the tip of a large iceberg of a storied musical tradition.

Son jarocho music has a vaunted history, which can be traced to the nineteenth century Spanish colonial era in Mexico, when it

Martha Vega Hernandez sings while rowing a boat in Boca de San Miguel, Veracruz, Mexico

was often performed by common people, farmers, and ranchers in the countryside.

Musicologists believe that elements of this practice go back even further, to the practices of indigenous people and communal traditions of West Africa.[4] The hand drumming that you find in African music can be heard in the dancing rhythms of *son jarocho* music. This type of music also became associated with feelings of resistance and struggle. During the eighteenth century, some of the *sons* or songs were banned because they were considered profane. For example, the song "El Chuchumbé," which can be traced to the West African term "cumbé" that means "dance," was forbidden because it refers to the loin area of the man, and the accompanying dance became

Martha Vega Hernandez and her granddaughter on a tarima in Boca de San Miguel, Veracruz, Mexico

one of courtship in which women lift their dresses.[5] *Son jarocho* music was performed by people of mixed colors and races. This mash-up of people performing music that was sexually provocative was too much for the Catholic Church, which held much power and sway over Mexico.

Since then, *son jarocho* has become more widely accepted and practiced in Veracruz and throughout Mexico. These days *son jarocho* has become a distinct music genre with specific practices and terms:

- *Son Jarocho*—Literally means "From Veracruz."
  This term has come to describe the music genre.

- *Fandango*—The communal event in which *son jarocho* is performed. The term *fandango* may be derived from *fandanguero*, which was once used to describe the summoning of devils through music; however this connotation has faded. People from the public gather to listen, feast, and revel at a *fandango*. Community members are encouraged to sing, strum, and step. Just like at a jam session among jazz musicians or *descarga* among Cuban musicians, there is an invitational spirit that welcomes everyone to contribute and enjoy the experience.

- *Jaraneros*—An artist who performs *son jarocho* music

- *Jarana*—A guitar, which comes in several sizes and can have as many as eight nylon strings. The *jarana* has a percussive, drum-like timbre when it's strummed vigorously.

- *Requinto*—Four-string guitar that is smaller than the *jarana* and is used to play the melody. This instrument also leads a *fandango*.

- *Leona*—Similar to a bass with four strings but it's tuned differently. Naturally, this is my favorite instrument because I play the four-string bass guitar. While in Tijuana, I played the *leona* during our recording sessions, and I didn't like the thought of ever putting it down.

- *Tarima*—A flat wooden platform on which there are one or two dancers (a man and woman, or two women). Every *son jarocho* musical performance is centered around the *tarima*. The music and festivities can't begin until the *tarima* is placed because of its focal role in the performance. All the singers and dancers are not necessarily on a stage with the audience looking at them. Rather, everyone gathers around the *tarima* and *jaraneros* to take part in the festivities.

- *Zapateado*—The term for the dance that is performed on the *tarima*. These dance steps are the central rhythm and beat of *son jarocho* music. They are accented and reinforced by the strumming of the *jaranas*, which creates a strongly propulsive and even repetitive feeling.

During a *fandango*, the *jaraneros* begin a *son* (song) with the lead singer who makes a *declaración* (declaration), which is followed by a *guitarra de*

Ramón Gutiérrez Hernández and Minerva Alejandra Velez dancing on the tarima in Xalapa, Veracruz, Mexico

son performed on one *jarana* that signals to everyone the actual piece that will be performed, from the meter and key, to the rhythm and overall vibe.[6] Whoever is the lead singer projects his or her voice, so they stand out prominently over the (at times) thunderous, instrumental accompaniment. The *jaraneros* take turns regarding who leads the *son*. But *fandangos* are usually led by the oldest or most experienced person.

The call-and-response format of the music gives *son jarocho* music a communal and collective aesthetic. Much of the music is improvisatory, there is no sheet music or even agreed order of what is to happen during a song, or how long it should last. Each piece evolves organically. There are typically only two chord changes, so almost anyone can strum along.

When I was at the Fandango Fronterizo in May 2018, several "non-musical" members of the production team, and my friends and family members, were playing the *jarana* and *leona*, and they were excited to be included. It's different standing on the side watching musicians perform versus being part of the actual music-making. When you're a practitioner, you're connected with your fellow artists, and you live in the moment. You're not on your smartphone recording the event—you are the event! Even though *son jarocho* is very much extemporaneous music, there is one thing that is planned. Every *fandango* begins with the classic and welcoming tune "El Siquisiri," the lyrics of which you can find in the appendix.

Because there is an emphasis on inclusion, *fandangos* have become events where relationships are formed and bonds are enhanced: "Reciprocity is expected and valued among *son jarocho* practitioners because it is a basic mechanism that enables the formation of tight networks of relationships," writes Alejandro Miranda Nieto, a musicologist.[7]

Despite what looks and sounds like an anything-goes jam session performance, there are complexities and intricacies to every performance. For example, younger *jaraneros* may defer to more seasoned performers, the order of tunes may be driven by the preferences of the dancers, or the host of the *fandango* may have views on how the music and overall event should come together. All of these subtleties are negotiated tacitly, on the fly, so that learning the "polite manners" of a *son jarocho* performance can take years to pick up.

Just as inclusion is encouraged, so too is patience: "*Fandangos* rarely have a peak-hour and there is no need to rush. There is space for everyone to sing if they want to, to pluck their stringed instruments, to step on the *tarima*, or simply to rest on a chair watching others doing it," writes Nieto.[8] A *fandango* typically begins with more upbeat numbers and then the repertoire becomes more peaceful and serene as the event goes on. For example, the song "El Buscapies" is usually performed after midnight because the lyrics are about a mysterious dancer on the *tarima* whose identity is revealed as the devil. *Jaraneros* then take turns singing verses to drive the devil away.

The musical repertoire of *fandango* is mostly composed of well-known *son jarocho* songs, the lyrics and translations of which you can find in the appendix. Many of these songs have sexual allusions. For example, the song "El Cascabel" is about the rattle of a rattlesnake. But a woman can sing about the rattle she wears around her neck, while claiming that she bought it herself—which means that she may be available to suitors. The suggestiveness of the lyrics reveals that there's more going on in *fandango* than you may first realize, especially if you don't speak Spanish.

Fandangos bring communities together, as they take days to prepare: Families and friends decide who will bring the food and beverages and which *jaraneros* will lead the music. They have to figure out who will bring the *tarima*. Some *fandangos* have been known to start in the evening and go on several hours, until the sun comes out the next day when it is easier to drive home. Though the *son jarocho* tradition originated in Mexico, it's celebrated throughout the Mexican diaspora and there are local *fandangos* that happen among this community, from Los Angeles to Las Vegas, and from Portland to Providence. For example, a group of *son jarocho* musicians holding workshops at venues like Citylore Gallery in the East Village in Manhattan charge around $10 to participate and take lessons. These events are attended by young and old people alike, from newcomers to seasoned veterans.

The *son jarocho* music and practices are mostly communicated orally at *fandangos* or workshops in which master performers share *sons*, lyrics, and techniques. Thus, to learn the intricacies of *son jarocho* can't adequately be done by reading about it in books or even watching clips online. You have to show up and jam!

Fandango Fronterizo

In 2008, a Chula Vista–based librarian, Jorge Francisco Castillo, began organizing a festival known as "Fandango Fronterizo" at the border wall between San Diego and Tijuana. Born in El Paso, Texas, Jorge grew up in Ciudad Juárez, Mexico. He is familiar with both

Kabir Sehgal, Humberto Manuel Flores Gutierrez, Arturo O'Farrill, Luis Villalobos, Alberto Villalobos during the Fandango Fronterizo

Jorge Francisco Castillo begins the Fandango Fronterizo Festival in 2018

countries, as he worked for many years in San Diego and now lives in Tijuana. He had volunteered to help clean up the beaches of Tijuana, an initiative that was organized by Daniel Watman, a local American. It was the first time that Jorge had been so close to this border wall, which became the staging ground for his eventual festival. After acquiring his first *jarana* in 2007, Jorge turned his sights on starting a festival, not as an overt political demonstration but one that celebrates commonality among friends, families, and community members who play and listen to *son jarocho* music on both sides of the wall. The event is very much a community event, and there are no giant corporate sponsors or performing strangers. It feels like friends throwing a block party. Now in its eleventh year, the event attracts a few hundred Americans who gather on the US side and Mexicans who meet at a plaza in Tijuana, and they peer through the tiny holes in the mesh to see and touch fingertips with those on the other side. They place two *tarimas*, one on the San Diego side, one on the Tijuana side. "When I saw the fence, and the people on the other side, I thought 'Wow, this is the perfect place for a fandango,'" he said.[9]

Organizing the event takes a considerable amount of time and effort. It requires obtaining a permit from the Department of Homeland Security (DHS) to stage the portion on the US side, and in today's political environment, this has become even more difficult, taking months to navigate the bureaucracy. In years past, US Border Patrol agents have been on hand to observe and monitor. But there are no political demonstrations or rioters—just a group of people singing and dancing *son jarocho*. There are recitations of poetry and improvisatory verses about the Fandango Fronterizo itself. A few celebrities like singer Aloe Blacc and his wife, rapper Maya Jupiter, have shown up, not as featured performers, but to listen, watch, and participate in the festivities. A group of local volunteers plan and organize the festival each year, from deciding who will bring what food, to which *son jarocho* artists to bring from Veracruz to lead the music. The festival typically takes place in the middle of the day and runs about four hours. Later that night, everyone gathers on the Tijuana side of the border, where there are a few concert-like performances, in which the likes of rapper Ana Tijoux have performed. An eight-hour *fandango* ensues with music, dancing, and even performances by puppets that reenact Mexican myths. People listen and jam, eat and drink, come and go.

During the evening festivities, it can be easy to forget about the animosity between both countries, because its people are celebrating their shared bonds, while the coastal breezes from the Tijuana beach cool the air. That there aren't feelings of hostility or resentment speaks to the importance of closeness and proximity. According to one survey, 57 percent of Americans who live close to the border have a positive view of Mexico, and 44 percent of Mexicans who are near the border have a favorable view of America compared to 28 percent who live in other parts of the country.[10] When you live close to someone, you get to know them better, and may even become less critical of them. But when you have distance from someone or some place, it can be easier to be disapproving or even derogatory.

Which is exactly the point of Fandango Fronterizo: to build bridges between Americans and Mexicans. This festival has succeeded in turning the wall from a symbol of division into a gathering place for artists, creative types, and members of the wider community. Its organizers are part of a larger group of artists and activists, on both the American and Mexican sides, who have turned the wall into a performance venue and art exhibition. The Mexican side of the wall is emblazoned with paintings and murals. Some of these images include the American flag, Our Lady of Guadalupe, a large jaguar indigenous to these parts, and a list of Mexicans who have served in the US military. "The art on the wall at the border is like a healing salve placed on an open wound…[it] invites one in and brings one up close, creating intimacy with the wall…one feels invited to altogether other vistas and ways of thinking. Transgressively, the art uses the wall to begin to undo the wall itself," write Edward Casey and Mary Watkins in *Up Against the Wall*.[11]

The values evoked by the Fandango Fronterizo are the same ones we wanted to reflect and dramatize in *Fandango at the Wall*. My musical

Arturo O'Farrill and the Afro Latin Jazz Orchestra perform with special guests in Tijuana in May 2018

partner, Arturo, came across a story about Jorge and his fellow festival organizers in *The New York Times*. After reading the piece, we thought it was grist for a new project. I couldn't find a website or email address for the festival or Jorge, and all the article said was that he was a librarian in the San Diego area. So I started calling libraries in the region. Finally, I reached his branch. The person who picked up the phone told me to call at 6 p.m. PST when Jorge would be leading a *son jarocho* workshop. Jorge called me back, and I later visited him and his colleagues during the Fandango Fronterizo festival in 2017 to see if he would like to collaborate on a multi-disciplinary project. And to our delight, he said yes.

Music Blurs Three Borders

Born in Mexico City, Arturo O'Farrill moved with his parents to
New York at age four in 1964. He lived his teenage years in the US
as an undocumented person, a "Dreamer" before the term took
on the meaning that it has today. In fact, Arturo didn't know his
status until he began performing music professionally and had to
travel to Europe for a show. When he went to apply for an American
passport, the clerk told him that he wasn't a citizen and that if he
left the country he wouldn't be permitted reentry. For the next ten
years, Arturo traveled with a Green Card, and he had to go to the
Mexican consulate in New York every year to get a waiver for the
mandatory military requirement that was obligatory for young
Mexican males. He eventually gained his citizenship, but the feeling
of being an "other" and not wholly legitimate viscerally shaped his
formative years.

Throughout his music career, Arturo has tried to use music as a cohesive force and even provocative device, to bring people and cultures
together, even when government officials say otherwise. For example,
in December 2014, Arturo and I traveled to Cuba to make an album
entitled *Cuba: The Conversation Continues* in which American and Cuban
musicians perform together. Just two days after we arrived, President
Barack Obama announced that the US and Cuba would resume
diplomatic relations. Our album became not just a musical piece but
a cultural statement that tried to capture the zeitgeist of reconciliation
that had enveloped the island country. As of 2018, our "Cuba" album
was the first "jazz" recording on the Delta Airlines in-flight entertainment system. We like to think that these sounds have helped acclimate
more to the sounds and people of Cuba.

In this same way, we hope that the music of *Fandango at the Wall* will help not only portray the same spirit but provoke people to think about folks on the other side of the border in a new light. Not as criminals, undocumented, colonialists, or imperialists. But as family and friends. Here is how Arturo puts it:

> For me, the *fandango* is touching because so many of its participants are family members who cannot physically hug but can only touch their fingertips to the mesh, and yet somehow they can feel fully connected to one another. They celebrate their musical heritage together, even though they're separated. I find music the most powerful way of connecting, so it's special that music is at the heart of this festival.

Arturo believed that it would be powerful to return to his birth country to perform a concert at the border wall. He hoped that such an event would serve as an act of goodwill and peace. In creating the music for this project, we had the goal of crossing (and blurring) three types of borders:

1. **Physical Borders**—recording musicians on both sides of the border wall.

2. **Musical Borders**—featuring *son jarocho* artists and also those from various countries, cultures, and genres. We aspired to pull down these man-made borders: rock, classical, jazz, rap, polka which are also human-made constructs. "The same twelve notes make up everything

you've heard, from John Coltrane to Johnny Cash. Music is music," said Arturo. To make this even more of a reality, we invited artists from so-called "banned" countries, those that hail from nations that were targeted in the executive orders of early 2017.

3. **Recording Borders**—blending sounds on the album between the rawness of live recording experiences with the pristine quality of a studio session.

First, we blurred the physical borders by recording musicians on both sides of the border. For example, during the Fandango Fronterizo festival, we recorded brothers Alberto Villalobos and Luis Villalobos on the Tijuana side of the border, and Ernesto Villalobos on the San Diego side. In addition, by holding recording sessions in Tijuana and New York, we wanted to send the message that music is what unites us, across barriers and borders.

To achieve the second objective, we included well-known *son jarocho* musicians from Veracruz and special guests from all around the world and who play many different genres of music. Here is more about the *son jarocho* musicians who joined us:

- **Patricio Hidalgo Belli**—A star *son jarocho* musician and for good reason. He has a velvet voice that will melt your heart and stay with you for days. He was born in Apixita, Veracruz, and is the grandson of Arcadio Hidalgo, one of the most iconic *son jarocho* musicians of the twentieth century. Patricio started playing the guitar when he was just a boy and has since followed the path that his grandfather blazed as a songwriter and master soloist. As a professional musician, Patricio has been a member of Grupo Mono Blanco; Grupo Chuchumbé; Grupo Quemayama; and Grupo Afro Jarocho, and he has recorded on at least six albums. He has also performed with Baroque ensembles and toured throughout Europe.

- **Ramón Gutiérrez Hernández**—He was raised in Tres Zapotes, Veracruz. At a young age, he was introduced to the *requinto*, which he has played for over thirty years. In his music, he is able to channel the great spirits of *son jarocho* veterans and masters, while also forging ahead and cultivating a modern sound. As an educator, he has taught workshops on *jarana, requinto, zapateado*. He has recorded at least twelve albums, five of which are with his group Son De Madera, which he started in 1992. And one of his albums was in collaboration with the Smithsonian. He collaborated on a project "Piano Xarocho" with a pianist that fused the music of Colombia and Venezuela with *son jarocho*. Ramón has also toured extensively throughout the US, from Seattle and Chicago to New York and Washington, DC. He has also toured throughout Latin America and Europe. He is a master luthier and builds his own instruments. He is currently based in Xalapa, Veracruz.

- **Tacho Utrera**—Born in El Hato, Veracruz, Tacho is a renaissance man: He is a talented musician, carpenter, and luthier who learned to make instruments from his father and grandfather. He plays the *leona*, *requinto*, and *jarana* and has enjoyed a thirty-year career as a *son jarocho* musician. Tacho has been a member of the bands Grupo Mono Blanco and Los Utrera. And during his career as a musician, he has toured the US, Latin America, and Europe, sharing the *son jarocho* tradition with the world. He has also recorded on several albums including "En el Hueco de un Laurel" and "Con Utrera yo Aprendí." Tacho is reserved and stoic but his music is soul-stirring. He is married to Wendy Cao Romero and has one son, Miguel Utrera, who is also a musician.

- **Wendy Cao Romero**—Her career as a *fandango* dancer began in 1987. She is a key member of the Utrera family, who promotes their artistry and shows throughout El Hato. In addition, she has produced numerous field recordings of older *son jarocho* musicians. She worked as a radio producer for thirteen years. As an educator, she has also put out a book that details the dance steps for *fandango* dancers. She attends and participates in *son jarocho* workshops. As part of her musical career, she has been a member of the Zacamandu group since 1992 and "Los Utrera" since 1993. She also plays the *jarana*. Beaming with a broad smile, Wendy infuses her performances with a buoyant personality. She teaches textile arts in El Hato "Mujeres Tejedoras," an organization of thirty women.

- **Fernando Guadarrama Olivera**—Hailing from Cordoba, Veracruz, he is an expert at performing ten-line verses known as "Decimas in *Son Jarocho*." The son of a physician, Fernando has lived in Oaxaca for nearly thirty years and has played the *jarana* for twenty-eight years. He has also taught poetry for *son jarocho* music for some twenty years. As an artist, he has toured poetry festivals throughout the US and Latin America. He also is the director of a poetry and *son* workshop in Tapacamino, Oaxaca, since 2005. His poetry has been extensively published and recorded. In October 2017, he performed at the fortieth anniversary concert for Grupo Mono Blanco at the Fine Arts Hall in Mexico City.

- **Martha Vega Hernandez**—Born in Salta Barranca, Veracruz, she is the daughter of legendary *requinto* performer Andres Vega Delfin. The oldest of nine siblings, Martha is a part of a family that has many accomplished musicians. When she was a girl, she started dancing in the city of Boca de San Miguel. She was also a member of Grupo Mono Blanco from 1984 to 1986 as a dancer. Martha is known as the best *zapateado* instructor in Veracruz and teaches workshops in the US and Mexico. Her sons Freddy and Claudio are members of the band Los Vega, which is located in Mexico City.

- **Zenen Zeferino**—Born in Jáltipan de Morelos, Veracruz, his family was made up of many musicians. He learned to play from his godfather. He plays the *jarana* and sings. He also writes his own poetry and songs. Known for his improvisations, he has developed a reputation as a master soloist. In 1992, he joined the band Chuchumbé with Patricio Hidalgo Belli and recorded albums *Caramba Niño* and *Contrapunteo*. He later formed the group Sonoro Sueño in 2009. Zenen has played an active role in reviving the *son jarocho* tradition. He now resides in New York, working with Radio Jarocho and other outlets to spread the music. He has toured around the world, including the Sydney Opera House with Jordi Savall. His family still lives in Veracruz.

Here is more information about the special guests who joined us and who represented other genres and traditions:

- **Regina Carter**—An accomplished jazz violinist who was born in Detroit. She studied at the New England Conservatory and has performed with the likes of Aretha Franklin, Billy Joel, and Max Roach. She became a MacArthur Fellow (also known as a "Genius" grant) in 2006.

- **Antonio Sanchez**—Born in Mexico City, Antonio is one of the most acclaimed drummers across all genres. He studied at the Berklee College of Music. He has won four Grammys, one of which was for the score that he wrote for the film *Birdman*. He also was nominated for a Golden Globe for his music on this film. He has released several albums that deal with the topic of immigration, including *Bad Hombre*.

- **Rahim AlHaj** (trio)—Born in Baghdad, Iraq, Rahim plays the oud, an instrument from the Middle East that looks like a lute and has between eleven and thirteen strings. He left Iraq after the Gulf War in 1991, and he became a refugee who settled in Albuquerque, New Mexico. He plays everywhere around the world, often with his trio which consists of Issa Malluff on the *cajons* (a type of drum) and Sourena Sefati on the santour, a hammered dulcimer instrument from the Middle East that has many strings. Rahim has a magnetic personality and had us all in stitches throughout the experience. He refers to himself as a "hummingbird" because he is always buzzing with ideas.

- **Sahba Motallebi**—Originally from Iran, she received her musical training at the Tehran Conservatory of Music. She plays the tar, a Middle Eastern string instrument that is strummed. She is also a talented songwriter and has toured all over the world.

- **Akua Dixon**—A renowned cellist from the US who has performed a range of styles from classical and jazz to world. She is a master soloist who has played alongside Dizzy Gillespie and Don Cherry.

- **Villalobos Brothers**—Ernesto, Alberto, and Luis are violinists and singers who come from Veracruz and now live in the US. They are three handsome and charismatic brothers that have infused *son jarocho* music with a modern, even hip aesthetic. They tour extensively with guitarist Humberto Manuel Flores Gutierrez.

- **Mandy Gonzalez**—She plays the role of Angelica Schuyler in the hit Broadway musical *Hamilton*. Previously, she starred in *In the Heights* and *Wicked*. Her family hails from Mexico.

- **Ana Tijoux**—A Grammy-nominated rapper who has mixed Chilean and French roots. Her family moved to France as political exiles during the reign of Augusto Pinochet, who was the president of Chile from 1974 to 1990.

- **Jose "Gurri" Gurria-Cardenas**—A composer and drummer from Mexico who leads his "Gurrisonic Orchestra." He studied at the Berklee College of Music and has performed with jazz luminaries such as Bob Mintzer and John Clayton.

- **Afro Latin Jazz Orchestra (ALJO)**—An eighteen-piece big band that is led by Arturo O'Farrill. The ensemble is composed of some of the most remarkable jazz musicians in the world, and you can see them play live every Sunday night at Birdland, a jazz club in New York.

Lastly, to achieve the third objective of blurring "recording borders," we recorded live and in-studio sessions. We conducted these live recordings:

1. May 25—Casa de la Cultura in Playas de Tijuana in which we recorded just the *son jarocho* musicians playing classic tunes.

2. May 26—Evening performance at the border wall by Arturo O'Farrill, the Afro Latin Jazz Orchestra, with special guests including the *son jarocho* musicians.

3. May 26—Fandango Fronterizo festival in which we recorded the revelry and music of the afternoon and nighttime *fandango*.

4. May 27—Casa de la Cultura in Playas de Tijuana in which we recorded Arturo O'Farrill, the Afro Latin Jazz Orchestra, and special guests including *son jarocho* musicians outside on the patio.

We also conducted an in-studio session at the Power Station in New York:

5. June 4, 5, 6—Arturo O'Farrill, the Afro Latin Jazz Orchestra, and special guests with Jorge Castillo and New York–based *son jarocho* musicians.

The Making of the Album

To prepare for our journey, Arturo and I listened to copious amounts of *son jarocho* music and traded playlists. "*Son jarocho* shows us how to come together and celebrate as a community. It helps us see a world without walls, borders, political ideologies, and even religion," observes Arturo.

Though our project is one of peace, our creative process is anything but. Arturo as the artist and I as the executive and artistic producer squabbled about repertoire and which guest artists to include. Our conversations got fierce. One of us finally decides to apologize to the other, and then we turn the page. Our disagreements aren't personal. It's just that we both believe ardently in the goals of the project. What's more, we marshaled a significant amount of money and resources to mobilize all the parts necessary to make this project happen. Yet we are resigned to the fact that jazz albums don't sell very much, and these projects only get done as labors of love.

With everything mostly in place, we reached Tijuana on May 24 and departed on May 27, 2018. As soon as we arrived, we went to the house of Jacob Hernandez and his partner Citali Canales, who help organize the Fandango Fronterizo, where he grilled meat while we were in the company of his pet tortoise named Lupe. A few of the *son jarocho* musicians started performing, and we all went upstairs to see them singing and dancing. It was the first time that Arturo had met Patricio, Ramón, Tacho, Wendy, Martha, and others. Regina and Akua were beaming as *son jarocho* music enveloped them. Issa started playing the *cajon,* and he sounded as if he had played *son jarocho* music his entire life, even though it was his first time! The *son jarocho* musicians gave him a few instructions in Spanish, and he nodded along, even though he didn't speak much of the language. It was a harbinger of the incredible time we would have during the festival and recording sessions, as we tried to communicate with those who were different, while also navigating the complexities of several cultural traditions.

That night everyone who was part of the project gathered at La Antigua Bodega de Papel, a local restaurant, to welcome one another. There was a lot of nervous energy in the air because we weren't sure quite what to expect, and many of the participants were meeting for the first time. I tried to keep the Tecates and Sols flowing! We ended the night with a production meeting in my room at the Dali Suites in which Arturo, our production team, and I met with the film crew to go over the game plan for the next days. We set up a WhatsApp group chat and started to communicate with each other, which we used to troubleshoot all the logistical issues, from who was responsible for transportation to what were the must-happen events of the subsequent day.

The documentary crew had recently returned from Veracruz, where they had spent time filming the *son jarocho* musicians in their home towns. They captured some of these musicians constructing their own instruments and singing solo pieces. My favorite scene was that of Martha, a sixty-three-year-old *son jarocho* singer and dancer, who was rowing a boat while singing. The footage was visually arresting, and Arturo and I were excited with what was in the works. Varda Bar-Kar led the film team, and I was impressed with her last film *Big Voice* about a high school choir instructor. Not only did she have experience making a music documentary, she had a brisk work tempo and responded to emails insanely quickly. Arturo and I decided to make a film just days before the event. I found Varda through a brilliant mutual friend, and she immediately took to the project and dove in with gusto, suggesting numerous creative and cinematic ideas. The first time that I met her in person was mid-stream, at the welcome dinner at La Antigua Bodega de Papel, while the project was underway. We had merged planning and execution into the same phase. I had known our director of photography, Matt Porwoll, for years. He won an Emmy for cinematography for his work on the 2015 documentary *Cartel Land*, in which he traveled with vigilantes patrolling the US-Mexico border. There were times when gunfire broke out while he was filming. He was glad to be back in Mexico as part of *Fandango at the Wall*, this time trying to document a more peaceful mission.

The next morning our first rehearsal began at the Casa de la Cultura in Playas de Tijuana with several of the *son jarocho* musicians blessing us with a song in which they seek and give permission. During the rehearsal, there was a lot of stress, as we tried to navigate technical problems such as equipment not working and the constantly changing schedules of everyone. When the *son jarocho* musicians said they had to leave in the afternoon for a workshop, I had to turn the rehearsal into a recording session, in order for us to capture "clean takes" of the music, so that it would match what was captured by the film crew in Veracruz (the music recorded there had a lot of ambient sounds like dogs barking and birds chirping). This meant stopping the rehearsal for several hours and working with our phenomenal engineer Rafa Sardina to improvise a recording session. Let's just say that not everyone was happy with me! After the long day, we left the Casa de la Cultura, the rehearsal space, and saw a beautiful dancing horse outside. The Villalobos brothers and ALJO members started to play their instruments, and everyone else was laughing and trying to capture the spectacle on their phones. It was just the moment of levity that we needed.

We took a van to the border wall at sunset. This was the first time that many members of the band had seen the barrier in person. Professor Douglas Brinkley joined us and shared a history of the border and discussed the politics surrounding the construction of the enhanced border wall. As we walked onto the Tijuana beach (and as the waves engulfed our shoes), he said that in the coming decades he thought the wall would become a relic and that the younger generation would find more ways to work together. We ended up in a roadside bar, where Arturo bought tequila shots with orange slices for the band!

The next day, on May 26, we took part in the Fandango Fronterizo festival, staged across the San Diego–Tijuana border. The DHS had limited the number of people who could participate in the *fandango* on the US side of the border to twenty at a time (and those who were waiting in line to join the *fandango* next to the border wall started another *fandango* just one hundred feet away on the US side). When I attended in 2017, there were easily over one hundred people, gathered in one place, on the US side of the border. The energy on each side of the border is quite striking. The US side has an area called Friendship Circle, an enclosed area that is adjacent to the Border Field state park. Despite its name, Friendship Circle is heavily patrolled with tall metal walls, and it feels foreboding because it's also in a remote location.

The Tijuana side is next to the main road, and there is bustling street life. The wall is decorated with images of brotherhood and sisterhood, symbols of indigenous wildlife, and an upside-down US flag. The festival was incredibly joyous, as ALJO members and special guests brought their instruments to jam with the *son jarocho* musicians. I could hear amazing flute and violin accompaniment during the festivities. I also made sure to grab the nearest *leona* and perform with everyone like the Villalobos Brothers, who were playing the violin. Antonio Sanchez was playing the *quijada de burro*, the jawbone of a donkey, which is a percussive instrument used in *son jarocho* music. While we were partaking in the event, the film crew was operating a drone to capture the overhead footage of the event and sharing the images in our WhatsApp group chat. It was remarkable to see how people were gathered around a symbol of division and turning it into one of unity.

Inspired by the spirit of this festival and its organizers, on the same evening, Arturo, the ALJO, several guest artists, and I performed a repertoire that fused Mexican and American traditions in Tijuana at the border wall. There was plenty of ambient noise: A Mariachi band was playing in the distance, and we waved our hellos to them; the lowrider festival was in town, with cars spinning their wheels (with plenty of engine smoke!) and making loud sounds; dogs barked loudly; people talked and laughed in the distance. We welcomed these street sounds and made sure to include them on the album. While we were waiting to begin, the band spontaneously began jamming together, and you could feel the energy starting to increase.

Despite not having power for much of the evening, the performance was electric, as we all had to listen closely to one other, and everyone grew with the moment. Arturo welcomed the audience in Spanish and spoke about the commonality of music. During the performance, our engineer Rafa whispered to me, "None of the mics are working," and that's when I started to play real loud because I knew any mistakes wouldn't make it on the recording! Thankfully (or maybe regretfully), we had some backup systems that recorded the event. The show was exhilarating and uplifting. A veritable jam session of music erupted and the crowd began chanting "*otro! otro!*" The entire band and *son jarocho* musicians jammed together on two final numbers: "El Cascabel" and "Conga Patria."

That the *son jarocho* musicians joined us was an incredible display of cross-genre artistry. For example, *son jarocho* musician Ramón Gutiérrez began soloing on the *jarana* on the piece "Fly Away" which has a Middle Eastern vibe. It was remarkable to watch a Mexican musician performing on a Middle Eastern song without compunction. But it isn't entirely surprising, considering that Iberian music draws upon these Arabic tonal and rhythmic influences, and Spain brought its musical traditions to the New World.

During the performance of "Amor Sin Fronteras" (Love Without Borders), a song dedicated to Dolores Huerta, an activist and contemporary of Cesar Chavez, I had to look down because I didn't want people to see my tears, as the moment struck me: musicians of many cultures, at the border wall, with the sun setting over the Pacific Ocean, as the audience cheered us on. After the performance, the nighttime Fandango Fronterizo festival kicked off. Arturo, ALJO members, family, friends, and I joined in the revelry and enjoyed making new friends at the event. Yet we didn't stay until the end of the *fandango* which ended at sunrise, as we trickled to our hotels to get rest and prepare for the recording session in the morning.

The subsequent day, we recorded many of the same songs from our border concert at the Casa de la Cultura, on the outside patio. Some of the songs like "Conga Patria" erupted into a full-fledged jam session where everyone started dancing. The musicians had to perform in the sun and we took breaks between each song to cool off. In the distance, we heard roosters, horses, and loud blasts that sounded like gunshots (there was a gun range nearby). Hummingbirds buzzed through the courtyard. We ate paella (non-vegetarian, to the chagrin of some band members) and popsicles. We drank iced coffee and water. We had a memorable day in which we tried to get through as much repertoire as we could.

After the session, I traveled across the border with my family who had joined me in Tijuana, and quickly found the closest In-N-Out Burger to have some comfort food. Before leaving, of course, I shared hugs with Arturo and Jorge, recognition of what had been accomplished but also knowing that we'll have to stick together to get everything done. There is always more work to do!

When I returned home to New York, I was determined to find a *leona* that I could play as part of the upcoming recording sessions. Jorge and Jacob put me in touch with some *son jarocho* musicians in the New York area, who I asked to borrow an instrument.

"Why don't you pick it up on Sunday at the event before your Monday recording session?" asked Paula, one of the local *son jarocho* musicians.

"What's happening on Sunday?" I asked.

"We hold a once-a-month *fandango* in New York. We have had one for fifty months in a row. This month we're hosting one in Rainey Park in the Bronx," she said.

"What a coincidence, I'm in the midst of this big *son jarocho* project..." I trailed off.

"It isn't a coincidence. This is what happens with *son jarocho*, when you bring people and friends together," she said.

After learning of the event, Jorge flew in from Tijuana. He, Arturo, Rahim, the Villalobos brothers, Sahba, Humberto, and more attended the *fandango* in the Bronx, where we met local *son jarocho* musicians such as Zenen Zeferino and Claudia Montes. We sang, strummed, and danced (even Arturo made a brief appearance on the

A fandango in the Bronx, New York

tarima!). After the *fandango*, Arturo and I invited them to Birdland to perform, and they all obliged. During Arturo's second set at the iconic jazz club, the *son jarocho* musicians performed riveting renditions of "El Cascabel" and "La Bamba" (complete with dancing on the *tarima*). Jorge observed that he had been in New York less than twenty-four hours, and he was already playing at Birdland!

On the next day, June 4, 2018, Arturo, ALJO, and several guest artists began a recording session at the Power Station studio in Midtown Manhattan. These sessions served as a mini-reunion, as many of the artists who joined us in Tijuana were also in the studio. By the time we laid down each track, we had played through the songs many times. In addition, we were joined by the likes of guest artist rapper Ana Tijoux, who delivered a captivating performance.

Arturo O'Farrill and the Afro Latin Jazz Orchestra with special guests record in the Power Station studio in June 2018

Mandy Gonzalez joined us on the last day, June 6, to sing two songs. Her father is a Mexican American who was a migrant laborer, and he was drafted to serve in Vietnam at age eighteen. "I learned how to totally, unequivocally, and enthusiastically embrace my culture. I learned when my agents early in my career 'encouraged' me to change my last name because it was 'too ethnic' to say NO," she said.[12] When she began singing, those of us in the studio booth were shaking our heads "yes" in admiration (we were also mouthing "DAYUM"). Her performance was a terrific capstone to wrap the recording.

As of this writing, we're planning to get the band back together, so to speak. We would like to stage a performance of the music we recorded at the border wall and on the album in a New York City concert venue. It would be incredible to see the *son jarocho* musicians like Patricio, Ramón, Wendy, Fernando, Martha, Tacho, Jorge, among others, join us as we bring the *fandango* to the Big Apple. It's a dream that I would like to see happen.

What did we record?

As of this writing, Arturo and I have heard only a few of the rough mixes of what we recorded. So, we're not quite sure what will make it on the actual album. What I can share is that, all told, I counted that we recorded eleven big band pieces, seven small group numbers, and fourteen *son jarocho* songs. Indeed, the music on this project comes from various genres and styles, and you can find the full repertoire listed in the book appendix:

Big Band: The centerpiece of the album is an original composition, the three-part big band "Invisible Suite" by O'Farrill, performed by

ALJO. The opus is partly inspired by the book *Invisible Cities* by Italo Calvino, an Italian novelist. The book is an extended conversation between Marco Polo and Kublai Khan, the Mongol emperor. Polo describes the various cities found across Khan's lands. The narrations serve as poignant commentaries not just about architecture but the foundations of history, modernity, and humanity. The text is as much about personal adventure as it is a journey to find the answers to many of life's most pressing questions such as "What is my purpose?" and "Who am I?" In chapters titled "Cities & Memories" and "Thin Cities" or "Hidden Cities" and "Continuous Cities," we learn about what makes each place unique, from those with soaring skyscrapers to those rural villages with endless nooks and crannies. All throughout, we hear of the differences and varieties of communities, yet the inhabitants make do with whatever situation in which they find themselves.

Arturo's "Invisible Suite" is a meditation on the co-existence of people, and how despite living in different places, we're inspired and motivated by many of the same things. His first movement is entitled "Invisible Cities." It juxtaposes the noises of the Mexican and American city streets with the silence you hear when you're at the top of a skyscraper. The altitude of distance can result not only in the divisions of people but the partitioning of minds. The piece begins with a person talking, and that voice is joined by a single instrument, followed by more accompaniment, to evoke the pitter-patter of street life. Here is when the main theme emerges, over an Afro-pop beat and rhythm.

The second movement is entitled "Free Falling Borderless." It was commissioned by the Young People's Chorus of New York City. It's a choir piece with evocative text by Eric Gamalinda. The piece features the Tijuana Youth Chorus known as "Cenzoltle," the name of a bird. The group recorded on the patio of the Casa de la Cultura in Playas de Tijuana. (Later they sang and danced to "El Cascabel," which was a beautiful and syncopated performance.) This third movement addresses the commonality of language, and how our mouths can only make so many sounds. For example, some of the same labial consonants that are used in French are found in Russian and Jamaican Patois. "This piece is about how we belong to the nation of the human being. We are members of a greater sisterhood and brotherhood of humanity. This is how we can use music to tear down walls," said Arturo.

The third movement is entitled "Invisible Beings." It's a piece that doesn't take itself too seriously. It sounds like lounge jazz with no pretension, as if you're just chilling with friends. All too often, we get caught up in our identities: our jobs, faiths, statuses, countries, and cultures. These things are no doubt important. But at the end of the day, we're all humans. And this song challenges us to discard all labels from "Anti-American" and "Anti-Mexican" to even "Mexican-American" and "American-Mexican." If you listen closely, this number pokes fun at people who can't laugh at themselves but gradually gives way to those who discover their true essence, with a middle solo section with rich harmonization.

The rest of the big band repertoire is also eclectic. One of the big band numbers is "Amor Sin Fronteras," written by Alberto Kreimerman, that was beautifully arranged by ALJO bassist Gregg August. The lyrics are about a Mexican national who travels to the US in search of a dream, and who has come to love two flags. Regina contributes a celestial violin part, which is so nimble and light, and makes you feel like you're drifting in the clouds. Mandy delivers an impassioned performance on this song too. "El Maquech" is a buoyant piece with a Mexican-sounding melody that repeats throughout. We performed it at the live concert at the border wall in Tijuana and it received a loud reception from the crowd. In addition, we recorded "Minotauro," a piece by Antonio Sanchez which is both calm and charged. The piece will slowly envelop you with bright cymbal work and propulsive rhythms. "Fly Away" and "Tabla Rasa" draw on tonal and rhythmic elements from the Middle East and South Asia. Hearing Rahim, Issa, Sourena, and Sahba featured on these works makes for an adventurous and uplifting musical experience. When Arturo mentioned that he wanted to include music from the Middle East, I was initially skeptical, and after listening to these songs, I agree with him. That's just another reason that Arturo is the maestro, and I'm merely the scribe! "Somos Sur" is a rap piece by Ana Tijoux, and

Fernando Guadarrama Olivera sings on train tracks in Minatitlán, Veracruz, Mexico

when we recorded this in New York, the session became a down-home groove session. Rocky, an ALJO trombonist, was swinging his head and arms in the air, while dancing to the groove. Every time Arturo would listen to the playback of the track in the session, he would also start to dance and throw his hands up with enjoyment. We also recorded "Jaiicasoebaim Noone," which is based on a field recording of indigenous people of the Sonora region. The piece was led by Adam O'Farrill, Arturo's youngest son. Finally, Gurri conducted and composed a number "Up Against the Wall" that blends *son jarocho* with an alarming, odd-meter feel. He's a talented and adventurous composer.

Small group: "El Pijul" and "Xalapa Bang" are tracks by the Villalobos that juxtapose their energetic vocals with blazing violin virtuosity. It's fun to see the three brothers singing their hearts out on these pieces. Regina, Arturo, Jorge, and a few others performed a small-group rendition of "Cielito Lindo," perhaps the most well-known classic tune in Mexico, which means "Lovely Sweet One." Mandy and Arturo also performed "Line in the Sand," which has emotional lyrics that personify the US and Mexico as friends or even lovers: "The stars look the same from where we are standing, Why can't we fix this mess we've made…" Rahim AlHaj trio recorded "Chant" and Sahba Motallebi recorded "Birth" on the spot during the New York sessions with no rehearsal time. In addition, a small group of ALJO musicians and New York–based *son jarocho* musicians recorded a piece that I helped create entitled "Hummingbird Blues," that is about these birds found in the borderlands. The song "Conga Patria" by Patricio Hidalgo might be the anthem for our project with the lyrics translating to "Wake up homeland, wake up!" The tune could be classified as *son jarocho* but every time he performed it, ALJO members would jump in! And for good reason: You can't resist this song. It makes you want to dance every time.

Son Jarocho—The film crew first recorded the *son jarocho* musicians singing these fourteen numbers in Veracruz, and we captured them again during our Tijuana sessions. You can find the lyrics of most of them in the appendix.

This music knows no borders because it speaks to the human spirit, and what we can accomplish together when we put aside our differences. Indeed, as history suggests, there will be many more ups and downs in the US-Mexican relationship in the decades to come. The buildup of the border wall may become a flashpoint for more rancor and acrimony. Xenophobia in the US and Mexico might increase as a result.

But when things sour between governments and diplomatic officials, it falls on private citizens to forge links and advance ties. It becomes the charge and arguably the responsibility of artists to provoke and sometimes even to subvert the world into one of amity and unity.

The people of the borderlands aren't waiting around to create this reality. This activist spirit has long characterized the people of the frontier. This time around, most aren't taking justice into their own hands. Some, including the organizers of Fandango Fronterizo, are rolling up their sleeves and creating visions of what friendship across the divide may look like. These industrious citizens are pouring their hearts and souls into creative endeavors, so that trans-border relations can one day become more in tune.

The takeaway here is straightforward: Think global but act local. This entire project began when a local librarian organized a festival at the border wall. Through his diligence and tenacity, he built something that brought together his community, and which can serve as a model for yours. You need not be a singer or dancer, a rapper or poet. But you already have an activist spirit that you can and should unleash into the world.

Americans and Mexicans live in a world in which we share not just friends and families but homes and habitats. Protecting these things that we have in common can serve as a cohesive force in bringing our people together more closely.

Patricio Hidalgo Belli with family in Minatitlán, Veracruz, Mexico

Tacho Utrera in his workshop in Consolapa, Veracruz, Mexico

Citali Canales dancing on the tarima at the border

Chapter 2

~~~~~~

REQUIEM FOR THE BORDERLANDS
How the wall would harm the environment

"A borderland is a vague and undetermined place created by the
emotional residue of an unnatural boundary."[1]
—GLORIA E. ANZALDÚA, poet and scholar

"We need to work together to maintain populations across the
international border at a certain level. The border is just a political
boundary; animals don't recognize it."[2]
—AARON FLESCH, conservation biologist

"The Tohono O'odham nation is my homeland.
I can never imagine a wall splitting my land in half."[3]
—HON'MANA SEUKTEOMA,
member of the Tohono O'odham people

Surely protecting the environment is a cause that both Americans
and Mexicans can support. Both nations share the borderlands,
and preserving these territories is a mutual responsibility, which neces-
sitates coordination and collaboration across both countries and their
communities. The nearly 2,000-mile border ranges between mountains and deserts to rivers and oceans. This all-terrain geography is
composed of several ecosystems made up of indigenous wildlife, from

pine oak forests and redwood flora to pygmy owls and jaguars. Within thirty miles of the border live at least 178 reptile, 134 mammal, and 57 amphibian species, according to a 2011 study.[4] To put this in perspective, these numbers account for 49 percent of the reptilian, 39 percent of the mammal, and 17 percent of the amphibian species throughout the US. Safeguarding this rich biodiversity is as much about actively learning about conservation efforts as it is restraining from overmining, overfishing, and overbuilding, especially constructing an edifice that impedes the migration of creatures big and small.

The existing border wall has already harmed indigenous wildlife. It bisects the populations and constrains the ranges of 152 reptiles, 113 mammals, and 38 amphibians that live near the border.[5] When a species has less room to move, an organism has fewer mating options, and it may start to inbreed with greater frequency, which results in a population with less genetic diversity, less resiliency to disease, and even increases their probability of extinction. The threat of this happening is more acute with smaller organisms with niche habitats, as their ranges are already narrow. In some cases, the border has cut the ranges for species as much as 75 percent.[6] Some of the 45 at-risk species include the western toad, sheep frog, rough green snake, Pacific pond turtle, Western fence lizard, Baja pocket mouse, and the Arizona gray squirrel.

The wall has also negatively impacted larger organisms. One study examining bighorn sheep found that the wall could hinder "connectivity of the metapopulation," thereby likely resulting in reduced genetic variety.[7] Bobcats have also had their populations confined: "Bobcats don't go out looking for holes in fences as they travel back and forth through brushy habitats. Overall, wildlife connectivity does not exist

Border wall extends into the Pacific Ocean

in these sectors anymore. I tracked some cats for a long time before the wall construction and did see significant shifts in territories," said Mitch Steinberg, a biologist.[8] He notes that because of the wall, two bobcats were trapped on one side, and they were eventually killed on a highway as they ranged for territory. "I'm afraid most of the previous bobcats are dead due to forced dispersal during construction."[9] Moreover, the wall has limited the capacity for bobcats and other large animals to obtain resources, like water, already scarce in a desert biome, which puts further pressure on populations.

The same can be said for jaguars, which have lost 54 percent of their roaming range since the early 1900s and have altogether vanished in parts of Central America.[10] These large creatures, which can be up to eight feet in length, pass through the borderlands under cover of heavy vegetation. They're an endangered and elusive species: Since 1996, only seven male jaguars have been seen, mostly by surveillance cameras. Despite their small numbers, they're apex predators, and thus important to regulating the ecosystem. If their population is reduced, there can be an increase in "mesopredators" like coyotes and other creatures that harm cattle owned by ranchers. "When you find a jaguar in one place, that means that ecosystem is complete, it's healthy," says Santa Napoles, who works with a non-profit organization.[11] Conservation biologists note that these creatures need large areas in which to roam. Jaguars in the US likely can't survive without being connected with those in Mexico. "A wall would eliminate that possibility," said Howard Quigley, the head of a big cat preservation program.[12]

Then there is the physical structure of the border wall itself. In parts of the Arizona border, the wall is nearly five meters or sixteen feet tall, which prevents pygmy owls from migrating. These creatures are typically seven inches high and weigh under three ounces. They fly low to the ground to avoid detection by potential attackers. One study found that just 23 percent of their flights exceeded four meters or thirteen feet in altitude, so the border wall inhibits their movement.[13] Because their flight paths have been impeded, their population further fragments, which can put more pressure on the overall species. "The tiny owls have never been more endangered than they are right now, because the border wall would inhibit their dispersal between Sonora and Arizona," concludes the Center for Biological Diversity.[14] In addition, near the border walls are bright tower lights that unnaturally illuminate the area that have caused "tower killings" in which birds crash into the wall, other edifices, or each other.[15]

In some cases, the wall has dammed running water, which leads to flooding and destruction of local habitats and ecosystems. This can also have negative consequences for humans. Tragically, in 2008, two people died in Mexico because of this type of flooding.[16] "A concrete wall that blocks trans-border water movement is a total obstruction…we are not in agreement with construction of a wall in the floodplain," said Antonio Rascón, head engineer for Mexico, with the International Boundary and Water Commission (IBWC).[17] He believes that the proposed wall would run afoul of the 1970 Boundary Treaty that demarcates the border between both countries, and which mandates that the IBWC must consent to any construction that impacts river flooding. "We are not in agreement with construction of a wall in the floodplain that affects the trans-border flow of water… we have been complaining about the fence since 1992…That's when they installed the first fence in San Diego, and it's been advancing and advancing," he said.[18]

These are just some of the consequences of the current border wall. A comprehensive study puts it simply: "New barriers would increase the number of species at risk."[19] With the most recent goal to construct barriers along 700 to 900 miles of the border, this threatens to cut across federally protected lands, wildlife reserves, and animal sanctuaries. Thankfully, the Santa Ana National Wildlife Refuge, composed of over 2,000 acres of land, near the Rio Grande River, was exempted from new wall construction by Congress in 2018.[20]

But other protected lands aren't so lucky. Five days after assuming the presidency, Trump issued an executive order that mandated building a border wall along the entire 2,000-mile-long border. He requested $23 billion in funding in 2018 but got $1.6 billion from

Congress, of which $38 million is intended for the wall.[21] These funds are earmarked for building more than 70 miles of new fences. The US Army Corps of Engineers is already conducting soil samples in wildlife sanctuaries in the Rio Grande Valley.[22] Some funding may also be used to build a second layer of fencing in the San Diego–Tijuana region, which is near the Tijuana Estuary that is home to marine life that could be negatively impacted by reducing the migratory flow of populations. Fish hatcheries, wetlands, and other ecosystems that are home to 111 endangered species could be at risk if the border wall is built in its entirety, according to the US Fish and Wildlife Service.[23] Another study says that the enhanced wall will harm 93 species and damage two million acres that serve as natural habitat for wildlife.[24] "The impact will be huge. It will be an environmental catastrophe," said Jeff Corwin, a conservation biologist.[25]

The border wall between Tijuana and San Diego goes into the Pacific Ocean

The proposed wall would cleave through 6,500 acres in southern Texas, according to a local environmental activist.[26] Some of these areas include La Parida Banco Refuge Tract, El Morillo Banco Refuge Tract, and the National Butterfly Center, which is a refuge for the monarchs, which are called *las palomas* ("the doves") by Mexicans, as these insects fly as much as 12 miles per hour, 46 miles a day, and at an altitude of 11,000 feet to reach a warmer climate in the south.

Not only would the wall have negative ecological consequences but also economic ones, as ecotourism, which generates $350 million and employs 4,407 jobs in the region, may suffer.[27] The Sabal Palm Sanctuary, located in the southern tip of Texas, experienced this firsthand when the number of visitors dropped after a border wall was constructed in the middle of it.[28] Surveyors and crews, toting chain saws, have already showed up at the National Butterfly Center to begin unblocking a path for a 38-mile fence, which may require the clearing of 30 million square feet of flora and fauna.[29] As a result, the center filed a lawsuit to prevent DHS from building the wall in these parts. "The center is private property…We believe the federal government has been behaving illegally and in a really egregious fashion," said the president of the North American Butterfly Association.[30]

However, the government can build and develop the borderlands with little to no compunction. One year before Congress passed the Secure Fences Act of 2006, it passed the Real ID Act, which was intended to strengthen the laws around identification so that driver's licenses, for example, could be used as official documentation. Some of the plane hijackers on September 11, 2001, used fake IDs, so the law created standards for identification cards. It also made it more difficult for undocumented immigrants to obtain IDs. One of the buried clauses gave the government the right to waive any laws it deemed necessary to erecting barriers and structures—like a border wall. The law permits the government to waive rules such as the Endangered Species Act, Wilderness Act, Clean Air Act, and Migratory Bird Treaty.[31] It also gave the secretary of the DHS the power to unilaterally make these decisions. What's more, it limited the ability of courts to review DHS decisions. Soon after the law was enacted, Michael Chertoff, DHS secretary, invoked his power. A federal district court had suspended the building of the border wall in southern Arizona because she found that the government hadn't conducted an environmental review. Chertoff waived several regulations so that the fence could be constructed near the San Pedro River.[32] All told, he issued a waiver five times, and the first two times were to permit wall construction near San Diego and in parts of Arizona. "We are trying to respect the substance of the environmental process and we are using the waiver authority where it looks like people are simply trying to stop or slow us down by throwing up procedural obstacles," he said.[33]

The DHS is now exercising this authority to enhance the border wall. Citing the 31,000 undocumented immigrants and 9,167 pounds of marijuana that border agents have seized in the San Diego sector since 2016, DHS issued a waiver to install secondary fencing over 14 miles in this region.[34] This will enable the government to put aside 37 laws and rules, including the Safe Drinking Water Act and Endangered Species Act. Despite several attempts to stop the government from waiving these rules, the federal courts have always found that DHS has the authority. Ironically, the same judge whom then-candidate Trump attacked for his Mexican heritage as being biased found in favor of the current administration, rejecting the challenge to the waivers by environmentalists.[35] Though the judge noted "the court cannot and does not consider whether underlying decisions to construct the border barriers are politically wise or prudent."[36] The Supreme Court hasn't weighed in on the matter officially, yet it has declined to hear cases that involve the dispute.[37]

Certainly, the government's authority to invoke eminent domain is enshrined in the Fifth Amendment of the Constitution. It will need to exercise this power if it wants to attain its goal of building the wall in full. As much as two-thirds of the borderlands isn't owned by the federal government but by states or the private sector.[38] The administration has sought two million dollars and twelve attorneys to deal with land purchases. It has expressed its interest in acquiring these lands by voluntary sale but not everyone will be inclined to give up their plots, as evidenced by those who own and maintain wildlife sanctuaries and preserves. And it's not just environmentalists who are resisting but plenty of folks who own properties that span the border. "Do they run the fence through the middle of my property?" asked Tony Zavaleta, whose ranch would be bisected by the wall.[39] Some five thousand properties in Texas are within a few hundred feet of the border, according to *USA Today*.[40]

Also, the indigenous people known as Tohono O'odham, which means "desert people," reside in the Sonoran Desert, on 2.7 million acres that traverse the border that was established by the Gadsden Purchase in 1853. Already, some 2,000 members of the group live apart from 32,000 others because the border runs through their community, so they have to use a tribal identification card to move between the US and Mexico. "This is Tohono O'odham land, and we've never been fully consulted on any policy," said Alex Soto, a member of the tribe.[41]

The proposed border wall would further constrain the "one people, two countries" people of the Tohono O'odham nation, who don't have a word for *wall* in their language but certainly have one for being peaceful: *dodolma.*[42]

Parks for Peace

Once upon a time, US and Mexican political leaders tried to turn the border into a symbol of peace, instead of a flashpoint of confrontation. In 1935, a US senator from Texas sent a letter to President Franklin D. Roosevelt suggesting the creation of an international park that spanned the border with Mexico. That same year, under Roosevelt's direction, officials from both sides met in El Paso, Texas, to sign an agreement expressing their intent to create a park in this region.[43] The secretary of state met with his Mexican counterparts to determine the policies and procedures that would govern the park. They set up a joint commission to provide recommendations for governments of both countries to consider and adopt. By 1936, the commission had determined the boundaries for sections of the park. Alas, the officials were inching toward a final accord when World War II broke out and interrupted their designs.

Following the creation of Big Bend National Park in Texas in 1944, Roosevelt was inspired to try again. He wrote a letter to Mexico's president Manuel Ávila Camacho: "I do not believe that this undertaking in the Big Bend will be complete until the entire park area in this region on both sides of the Rio Grande forms one great international park."[44] In response, Camacho consented with Roosevelt's plan to resume the formation of the common greenspace. But this required Mexico to establish its section of the proposed park, and to protect all the territories that were contiguous with Big Bend National Park, which would take time to implement across Mexico's governmental bureaucracy. After Roosevelt died, President Harry Truman took up the mantle and wrote Camacho to revive the plan.[45] But the conversations ultimately stalled in the 1950s, as not all of the adjoining lands in Mexico were given protected status. In addition, during this period, both governments revisited whether the park was in each country's self-interest, as the alliance and collaboration of the war years was eclipsed by the mutual skepticism and antagonism of the post-war decades.[46]

The shared interest picked up again in the 1980s when the head of Big Bend National Park in the US pursued the idea with the governor of Coahuila, the Mexican state adjacent to Big Bend. Several local and even regional officials made attempts at unifying the lands and realizing the international vision, from the local rotary associations to outdoorsmen wanting to safeguard the environment. In 1994, the Mexican government deemed some of the territories opposite Big Bend National Park protected but still not all. Meanwhile, the US and Mexico federal governments created a patchwork of principles and frameworks for agreements to foster collaboration and conservation across the border to create the "Big Bend Rio Bravo International Park" that could have included such beautiful areas as the Maderas del Carmen and Cañón de Santa Elena in Coahuila. But to be sure, both governments have historically cited impediments to realizing the vision, from not having a sufficient amount of bilingual staff to how to transfer funds among entities charged with overseeing an international park.[47] Some have floated the concept of creating "sister parks" instead of a fully international and integrated park, to catalyze an agreement.[48]

In 2009, President Felipe Calderón of Mexico gave the Ocampo area protected status, which finally created lands that adjoined Big Bend National Park and safeguarded it. In 2010, congressman Ciro Rodriguez of Texas introduced a bill to create the international park at Big Bend that would include 3 million acres of land, which would have accounted for 14 percent of the border. It would be home to at least 3,600 species of insects and 446 species of birds.[49] But in the post–September 11 climate, it was difficult to pass anything that seemed to loosen the border, or that could be perceived as encouraging undocumented immigration or opening the door to a wave of violence unleashed by the Mexican War on Drugs. "I have to admit the timing is not appropriate, given what's happening in Mexico, but I'm optimistic we'll get past this in time," he said.[50] Even though DHS planned to up the number of border patrol agents and to increase security measures at checkpoints, critics didn't feel like it was enough.

After the Gulf of Mexico oil spill in April 2010, the plans to establish the park were set aside. US Department of the Interior officials had to tend to resolving this environmental catastrophe, and the political will for an international Big Bend receded. "Here this project is over 70 years old and up until 10 to 20 years ago, the main problem was Mexico was distrustful of us and now that they trust us, the problem in making it happen is on our side of border," said an environmental activist in El Paso.[51]

Just like a *fandango*, a shared park is an alternate vision to the border wall. It's also a refreshing reminder that the human-made border is just that—a line of demarcation that separates people and places. A wall upsets the natural order of things, but a park is a place where animals can roam relatively freely, and ultimately inspire us to live in a world in which more people can think and move without compunction. A park is a place that relies on mutual trust and respect. We could use more of these concepts and models to help us see folks across the border not as criminals or enemies or even familiar strangers, but those with whom we share ancestors and friends, interests and leisure activities.

It's important to emphasize the commonality of the borderlands because for nearly two hundred years, the border has served as a flashpoint. When you put the current diplomatic row into its historical context, it becomes apparent that the struggle to bring peace to these lands is evergreen.

*Arturo O'Farrill and the Afro Latin Jazz Orchestra with special guests record
at the Casa de la Cultura at Playas de Tijuana in May 2018*

The Afro Latin Jazz Orchestra performance at the border wall

The dancing horse that captured our imagination outside the Casa de la Cultura in Tijuana. Members of the band serenaded the horse with music.

Chapter 3

BRICK BY BRICK

A short history of the border and wall

"On paper one easily draws a line with a ruler and pencil;
but on land it is not the same."
—MEXICAN SURVEYOR with the Joint United States
Mexican Boundary Commission[1]

"Texas will again lift its head and stand among the nations.
It ought to do so, for no country upon the globe can compare
with it in natural advantages."[2]
—SAMUEL HOUSTON, first president of Texas

"My sole ambition is to rid Mexico of the class that has
oppressed her and give the people a chance to know what
real liberty means. And if I could bring that about today
by giving up my life, I would do it gladly."[3]
—PANCHO VILLA, Mexican general

The Border

The US-Mexico border, as we know it, was created over a period of roughly fifty years starting in the 1820s: "In five decades, the border had changed from no border to an imaginary border to a disputed border to a negotiated border to a line on a map," writes *USA Today*.[4] The key agreements and events that shaped much of the border include: (1) the Transcontinental Treaty, (2) Mexican Independence, (3) the Texas Revolution, (4) the Mexican-American War, and (5) the Gadsden Purchase.

In 1819, the Transcontinental Treaty, which is also known as the Adams-Onís Treaty (named after the then US secretary of state and Spanish foreign minister), was agreed upon by the US and Spain. At the time, Spain was a colonial power in the midst of a war against Mexico, which was fighting for its independence. The treaty established a border between US territories obtained via the Louisiana Purchase in 1803 and the adjacent Spanish lands. It drew a border that started in Southwestern Louisiana and extended west in line with 42° latitude toward the Pacific Ocean.[5] As part of the deal, Spain relinquished Florida, which had become unruly with settlers and Seminoles competing for land and interests. In exchange, the US gave up parts of what are now Arizona, Texas, New Mexico, Nevada, and California.[6]

When Mexico won its eleven-year war for independence in 1821, it assumed much of the land ruled by Spain, from the Rocky Mountains to the Yucatan Peninsula. Mexican officials believed that their extensive terrain would one day yield significant resources and assets. But after three hundred years of Spanish rule, the "Mexican Empire," as it was then called, was beset by internecine conflict as various factions struggled to assume and maintain power let alone marshal resources to develop the hinterlands. With the power and economic resources concentrated in Mexico City, the remote borderlands to the north suffered with little investment, oversight, or even stability, as Apache tribes stormed Mexican encampments. Meanwhile, many American settlers migrated to these lands in large numbers, and they quickly outnumbered Mexicans in Texas in the late 1820s.[7]

Immigration would become the root of the first armed conflict between the two countries. In 1830, Mexico banned American immigrants from moving to Texas. According to the eleventh article of this law:

> It is prohibited that emigrants, from nations bordering on this republic shall settle in the states or territory adjacent to their own nation. Consequently, all contracts not already completed and not in harmony with this law are suspended.[8]

To restate this point: Mexico banned *American* illegal immigrants. On one occasion, a Mexican military officer came across American nationals without a passport, so he demanded they leave: "As they have come into this country contrary to law and have disrespected the authorities, I think they ought not to be admitted," he wrote.[9] In an effort to discourage American settlers, Mexico banned slavery, increased tariffs on American goods, and increased taxes. Mexico gave preferential treatment to its citizens who moved to Texas, providing them better plots of land and financial support.

But the Americans kept coming. Meanwhile, in 1835, President Antonio López de Santa Anna of Mexico rescinded his country's constitution, a move that gave him more control over the government and power over the borderlands. Santa Anna's usurpation of power further exacerbated relations with the Americans, who were already wary of the anti-American measures and laws. The settlers eventually started the Texas Revolution, in which "Texians" took up arms against the Mexicans in autumn 1835. Mexican officials were suspicious of America's role in the rebellion, as they believed the US government, which had broached the topic of redrawing the American borders to include Texas in 1826, had initiated the revolt to eventually annex Texas. The Mexican army under the command of President Santa Anna initially quelled the insurrection, as it felled the Texians at the Battle of the Alamo in 1836. But the Texians pressed on, declared their independence as a republic and, under the leadership of army commander Sam Houston, won the war against Mexico in 1836. The US later annexed Texas as the twenty-eighth state in 1845, which pushed the American border south into what Mexico considered its territory.

But Americans didn't want to just expand southward. They also wanted to push westward toward the Pacific Ocean. They aspired to spread their country's borders from coast to coast to secure disputed territories, advance its economic interests, and win more legitimacy as a nation state from European countries that still considered America as a backwater or experiment. This belief in "manifest destiny" animated settlers and American officials alike. President James Polk came to power on an expansionist platform in 1845, and he offered to purchase New Mexico and California from Mexico in the same year. He also wanted to establish the Rio Grande River as the border between the two countries, which would make Texas fully part of the US.[10] Mexico was ill prepared to consider or negotiate the proposition, let alone fight a war, as its presidency had turned over several times by that point, and because political factions struggled for power and legitimacy.

Border wall between Tijuana and San Diego

Nevertheless, Mexico rebuffed the US offer, and President Polk responded by sending troops under the command of General Zachary Taylor to the disputed lands near the Rio Grande River. The presence of US forces inevitably provoked an attack by Mexican soldiers in April 1846, and therefore established the *casus belli* for both sides, and the Mexican-American War began. Citing the violence, President Polk obtained a declaration of war from Congress. US military forces fought without compunction, and waged battles from the Rio Grande corridor to Baja, California.

The US won the war, and it ended with the signing of the Treaty of Guadalupe Hidalgo in 1848, in which the US paid Mexico $15 million, and established the Rio Grande River as a permanent border between the two countries. In a stinging defeat, Mexico lost more than 50 percent of its territory and ceded California and parts of Arizona and New Mexico, as well as territories farther north such as Colorado and Wyoming. There were even calls in America to annex all of Mexico. The border west of the Rio Grande River was drawn as a straight line by American diplomats and "was made up of a series of imaginary lines," writes historian Rachel St. John.[11] "The delineation of the western half of the boundary line created an entirely new space in the west...there had simply been no *there* there before the Treaty," she concludes.[12]

Moreover, little attention was given to the actual inhabitants of these disputed lands, and American officials were nervous about including too many Mexicans in its newly obtained territories. Meanwhile, Mexico maintained that it should retain some of these lands because the residents were ethnically and culturally Mexican. But with US military forces occupying Mexico City, Mexican officials had little room to negotiate.

Though the treaty made clear where the border was on the map, it remained difficult for surveyors to demarcate the actual lands because of geography, weather, and indigenous people. As a result, during the mid-nineteenth century, sections of the borderlands were practically still in dispute, particularly the areas in what's now southern Arizona and New Mexico. The US wanted to secure this region so that it could build a faster train route to link east and western lands, and to abet trade and commerce. In what became known as the "Gadsden Purchase" after James Gadsden, the US ambassador to Mexico, the US bought roughly 30,000 square miles of land from Mexico for $10 million in 1853. Still reeling from the loss of its lands to the US and needing to bolster its finances, the Mexican government accepted the offer. According to the US State Department, the deal created the southern border of the US, and it was the last major land amendment between the two countries.[13] To be sure, certain areas of the border like the Rio Grande corridor were still in dispute, unresolved until the Boundary Treaty of 1970. But with the Gadsden Purchase, the border as we know it had mostly been established.

The Wall

Protecting the border is another topic altogether. There wasn't a border or fence during the 1800s.[14] Rather, Mexicans and Americans traversed the border relatively freely, fearing not government patrols but local vigilantes, Apache warriors, or foreign mercenaries. The "Wild West" power dynamics were constantly in flux, and who was in charge locally was more important to one's survival than respecting national boundaries.

Despite its remoteness, the borderlands attracted plucky entrepreneurs and investors in search of metals, minerals, and other natural resources. This "transnational capitalism" attracted Americans and Mexicans to this region looking for jobs and opportunities.[15] As a result, the population of these lands swelled in the late nineteenth century and further blurred the border.

In the 1890s, the US and Mexican governments needed to get a better handle on identifying who was who, and what goods they could tax, so they created several entry ports and established border monuments to demarcate the line of control. A boundary commission recommended a strip of land fifty feet wide on both sides of the border in which building was prohibited, and President William

Arturo O'Farrill and Luis Villalobos at the wall

McKinley issued a proclamation in 1897 that implemented this zone in Nogales, Arizona. Local businesses and residents moved to their respective sides, and the border started to take on real meaning as a dividing line between two nation states.

It also became a line of control. At the turn of the twentieth century, US border patrols started to restrict migrants, particularly those from China. Because of the mid-nineteenth-century gold rush and building of the transcontinental railways, many Chinese had moved to America to work as laborers for low wages, and they ended up settling in enclaves throughout the US. In 1882, the US enacted the Chinese Exclusion Act that banned Chinese immigrants, but they eventually found another route into the country, through Mexico. The Bureau of Immigration in Washington, DC, dispatched inspectors or "line riders" to the borderlands to curb Chinese migrants and Mexican nationals.[16]

With border patrol agents on the lookout, smuggling took off. Intrepid residents operated trafficking routes across the border and even bribed agents not to interfere. While in Mexico, Chinese were relatively free to remain and become citizens, but when they crossed the border, they were subject to arrest and deportation back to Mexico or China.[17] In order to combat smuggling, the US Border Patrol received more resources to augment their presence.

Armed patrol agents became a more constant presence around the same time as the Mexican Revolution, which broke out in 1910, ending a thirty-year-long rule of the country's then dictator Porfirio Díaz, whose policies favored the wealthy. The ten-year struggle claimed the lives of as many as two million Mexicans. The nation increasingly militarized its border, and its army turned many of its checkpoints into fortified installations, where they could more aggressively collect taxes and duties that would finance military operations.[18]

Violence also spilled over the border. Infuriated that the US had supported his adversaries, Mexican Revolutionary General Francisco "Pancho" Villa raided Columbus, New Mexico, and killed seventeen Americans in 1916. His brutality elicited a furious response from President Woodrow Wilson, who dispatched several thousand troops under the command of General John Pershing to capture Villa. In what became known as the "Border War," these American forces entered Mexico and fought periodic battles with rebels but ultimately were not able to catch the elusive Villa. Though the US forces returned home in 1917, the memories of war lingered, as did the mistrust, suspicion, and heightened military presence on both sides of the border.

It's with this backdrop of mutual skepticism that the US intercepted the Zimmermann Telegram. In 1917, during World War II, Arthur Zimmermann, an official at Germany's foreign affairs ministry, sent a correspondence to the German ambassador in Mexico to make a proposal to the Mexican government: In exchange for Mexico attacking the United States, Germany would restore Mexico's territories it had lost to the US. This communication precipitated a national outrage in America, and the US soon declared war on Germany. American customs agents scrutinized goods more closely that were crossing the border with Mexico. For example, they prohibited German propaganda films from being sent to Mexico.

Meanwhile, the border was hardening with more fences and walls. In 1909, the first border fence was erected not to limit human migrants but the movement of animals. At the time, cattle ranching was a hot-button issue because Texas fever ticks had been eradicated on the American side of the border but not the Mexican.[19] The fence was installed by the Bureau of Animal Industry in Baja, California, to restrict the movement of cattle carrying ticks.[20] Throughout the 1910s and 1920s, the US and Mexico installed more fences to regulate animal movements, and increasingly smugglers and migrants. By the mid-1930s, more barbed wire fences had gone up, as a result of the International Boundary and Water Commission, which wanted to further restrict the movement of cattle. As for limiting the number of immigrants, the US officials expanded a chain link fence in Calexico, California, to run for nearly six miles in the 1940s.[21] "By the 1980s, although immigrants and smugglers cut holes in the chain link and most fences consisted of only a few stands of barbed wire meant to keep out nothing more than cattle, fences marked much of the border," writes St. John.[22]

In response to concerns about heightened drug use in America, St. John points out that fence-building became more rigorous during President Bill Clinton's administration in 1994 with "Operation Gatekeeper." This initiative placed special focus on the San Diego sector, one of the many sectors monitored by border patrol agents. It elongated the border wall in this sector some 136 percent, from nineteen to forty-five miles. In addition, hundreds of sensors and thousands of border patrol agents were placed at the border. These measures helped to reduce the number of undocumented immigrant crossings by 75 percent in this region, according to the US Customs and Border Protection.[23] By 2000, only sixty miles of the border had fencing, mostly around the San Diego area.[24] Another initiative, "Operation Hold the Line," was launched in 1993 near El Paso, Texas, and similar measures were introduced that also helped to reduce the number of apprehensions, as fewer people likely attempted to cross.

The most rigorous buildup of the border wall came in the years after the terrorist attacks on September 11, 2001, as US officials sought to better safeguard the homeland. The Secure Fences Act of 2006, which had bipartisan support, was enacted under President George W. Bush's administration. "Ours is a nation of immigrants. We're also a nation of law. Unfortunately, the US has not been in complete control of its border for decades," said Bush upon signing the bill.[25] Due to the law, border security funding increased from $4.6 billion in 2001 to $10.4 billion in 2006. The number of border patrol agents increased, members of the National Guard were deployed to the border, and more detention centers were established.[26] The law also created nearly 650 miles of new border walls and fences, which reportedly cost $2.3 billion or perhaps as much as $16 million per mile, with billions more needed to maintain these dividers. These walls are made of steel, wire, concrete, and even repurposed military air strips and pontoon bridges.[27]

In response to the law, President Felipe Calderón of Mexico said, "Humanity made a huge mistake by building the Berlin Wall, and I believe that today the United States is committing a grave error in building the wall on our border."[28] Yet, the goals of the bill weren't to please Mexican officials. The intent was to stem migration, and that's arguably what it achieved. The law may have had a considerable effect on reducing the quantity of apprehensions of undocumented persons. For example, in 2007 the total number of apprehensions dropped to 858,722, from over one million in 2006.[29] The wall hadn't been built, but the message had been sent: The US was getting serious about limiting Mexican immigrants. Even though sections of the wall eventually went up, new smuggling routes emerged, such as underground tunnels and passageways. And the wall was still permeable, as migrants could scale or cut through it.

The border is indeed long, winding, and porous. It runs approximately 1,954 miles from the Gulf of Mexico in the east to the Pacific Ocean in the west.[30] It spans four American and six Mexican states and dozens of municipalities. As much as two-thirds of the border traces along the Rio Grande River.[31] As of 2017, some 650 miles or 20 percent of the border had a non-contiguous dividing wall or fence, tracking parts of California, Arizona, New Mexico, and western Texas. And about half of these 650 miles have a wall that is intended to stop only automobiles, not those journeying by foot, according to *USA Today*. This leaves just 350 miles or 17 percent of the border shielded by a divider meant to stop foot travelers.[32] To be sure, the border isn't protected by just a wall and barbed wire but thousands of guards, virtual fences, cameras, and drones that watch from above. Even still, border hawks have called for two layers of fencing throughout the border.

As of 2018, Trump had instructed homeland security officials to obtain prototypes for transparent walls that are eighteen to thirty feet high. Yet it's unclear how long the wall would run. Even Trump lowered expectations, saying: "You don't need two thousand miles of wall because you have a lot of natural barriers...mountains...rivers that are violent and vicious."[33] Even still, some estimate that his border wall may range from 700 to 900 miles. The costs of building such a wall are not estimated easily. According to a DHS report, it will cost $21.6 billion to construct, but not factored in are all the transportation costs to move materials, and legal fees because the government doesn't own all lands that a wall would cut through (and would have to invoke eminent domain)—not to mention the billions needed to maintain the wall over the years to come.[34] An MIT estimate projects the border wall will cost as much as $40 billion, with around $9 billion just for concrete. And Congress has yet to provide the $33 billion requested for the border wall either. If the funding materialized, it would still take at least seven years, in the best case, to construct the wall.[35]

The border isn't impervious, as the stream of Mexican nationals continues to show. That a more hardened and impenetrable divider doesn't exist after more than two hundred years of shared history between the US and Mexico speaks to the difficulty and complexity of building such a structure. Just as there have long been concerns and calls to harden these lands, from engaging in more aggressive patrols in the 1940s to erecting permanent walls in the 1990s, there have also been mitigating forces: intertwined relations of people and businesses in the region, as well as the priorities and political will of local, state, and federal officials. There have always been questions about who is going to pay for security measures and how much they will cost. But the prevailing reason for why a more fortified border hasn't materialized might be because of geography. The large expanse of borderlands is remote, rugged, and rocky—as well as wet, watery, and wild. Because of this meandering terrain, for much of its history the border has been unwieldy, regulated by frontiersmen, tribesmen, and vigilantes who took measures into their own hands.

Certainly, the border has been forged in the crucible of many conflicts. And it's only natural for nations to want to secure and defend their own borders with measures they deem fit, from checkpoints and guards to fences and roadblocks. But when the president consistently explains his preferred policy proposals with inflammatory rhetoric that distorts and stereotypes a group of people, he ends up building another type of wall entirely, which also has plenty of historical precedents.

Fandango Fronterizo Festival in 2018

Chapter 4

THE MENTAL DAM
A short study of xenophobia in Mexico and the US

"American history is longer, larger, more various, more beautiful, and more terrible than anything anyone has ever said about it."[1]
—JAMES BALDWIN, American novelist

"America is under siege, facing a hostile invasion on its own soil… The invaders are ILLEGAL IMMIGRANTS, their battleground is the US-Mexico border, what's at stake is the money, security, and freedom of all Americans."[2]
—JON E. DOUGHERTY, American author

"We [Mexicans] are not people of merchants and adventurers, scum and refuse of all countries, whose only mission is to usurp the property of miserable Indians."[3]
—LUCAS ALAMÁN, Mexican author

In recent years, the US-Mexico relationship has become marked by mutual skepticism, antagonism, and even contempt. In response to President Trump's fiery rhetoric and hardline policies, Mexican officials have harshly criticized America and those who hold seemingly anti-Mexican views.

In the run-up to the 2018 Mexican presidential elections, Andrés Manuel López Obrador (known by his initials AMLO), who ran on the left-wing MORENA party ticket (and ultimately won the presidency), pulled no punches, citing "the discourse of hate and viciousness against foreigners that enabled" the current US president to win.[4] In that same speech that he delivered in Los Angeles in February 2017, AMLO took his own rhetoric up a notch, comparing the ascendancy of certain ideas in America with that of the Third Reich:

> These smart though irresponsible neo-fascist people now in power want to build walls in order to turn the United States into a huge ghetto and compare Mexicans in general, and our migrant countrymen, specifically, with the Jewish people who were stigmatized and persecuted in Hitler's era.[5]

Indeed, AMLO has been a long time detractor of America and, most notably, its foreign policy toward Mexico. Not wanting to be outdone, his competitor Ricardo Anaya Cortés of the PAN party also delivered a speech in California in which he criticized Trump and his policies.[6] Even the more buttoned-up and conservative candidate José Antonio Meade, who ran on the PRI ticket, affirmed "Mexico demands respect" in a video message addressed to the US president.[7] If there is one thing that Mexican politicians from all parties can agree on, it is that the rhetoric and policies coming from America must be denounced and rejected.

These politicians are reflecting popular opinion: In 2015, some 66 percent of Mexicans held positive views and 29 percent had negative views of the US. But in 2017, the numbers reversed with 65 percent of Mexicans holding a disapproving view with only 30 percent with a

The border wall between Tijuana and San Diego

positive outlook. Some 85 percent of Mexicans have a negative opinion of Trump.[8] What is more, in Mexico these negative sentiments have devolved into episodes of burning the American flag and hitting piñatas of the American president.[9] One protester carried a picture of Trump with a grim Hitler mustache with the inscription "Twitler." Others held up a sign that read "Make America Hate Again."[10]

But to say that the negative sentiment between the two countries is a new phenomenon isn't accurate. The relationship between Mexico and the US has been fraught with over two hundred years of back-and-forth amid peace and war, marked by love and hate between friend and foe. If anything, the recent turn toward mutual antagonism and heightened xenophobia is a reversion to the mean, return to normal, and resumption of a historical row, after years of rapprochement.

This chapter briefly examines past examples of the resentment that has beset these two countries. It will help place into context the current diplomatic dispute between Mexico and the US. By no means should we accept or brush aside the negative turn in trans-border relations as just the latest swing in a troubled association. Instead, we should be mindful that if left unchecked, xenophobia can worsen into conflict and violence. That US immigration officials are separating families at the border in June 2018 is a recent example of hard-line policies triumphing over basic decency and humanity.

Alas, intolerance never vanishes completely: "It recedes from prominence, and makes regular unwelcome returns,"[11] writes Professor R. R. Sundstrom of the University of San Francisco. Walls aren't built just on borders but *within* countries, communities, and classrooms. And even between friends and families. These mental dividers aren't constructed with bricks but neurons that wire together to form biases, prejudices, racism, and tribalism.

Fearing the Gringo

Decrying Americans as colonialists, imperialists, and *gringos*, Mexicans have long looked upon their northern neighbors with suspicion and scorn. Though Mexico may have been a weak state with battling factions during the nineteenth century, their shared resentment of America served as a cohesive force and intensified feelings of Mexican nationalism.

Until this day, many believe that the US has committed a litany of geopolitical wrongdoings, from the Mexican-American War, to the recent militarization of the border. That Mexico ceded half its land to America after the war is surely cause for misgivings. On several occasions, US military forces have invaded and occupied Mexico, which has stoked vehement anti-Americanism among its people. Mexicans have also resented US businesses that have bought vast tracts of borderlands and legally, and in some cases, illegally, tapped the oil and gas fields in the Gulf of Mexico. More recently, Mexicans boycotted American coffee maker Starbucks, and sales dropped 9 percent in the quarter after Trump's inauguration.[12] Indeed, anti-Americanism in Mexico remains a trenchant force today.

But let's revisit one period of severe anti-Americanism to render a fuller historical portrait of xenophobia in Mexico. During the Mexican Revolution, from 1910 to 1920, the country endured a chaotic era in which various factions competed for power. It was also a period of American interventionism, as the US used economic, political, and military means to gain more power and influence over Mexico. Such overreach validated Mexican fears of the *gringo* imperialists and further exacerbated the relations between both countries.

It's with these circumstances that the events of November 1910 combusted into full-fledged anti-American riots. An angry mob in Rock Springs, Texas, lynched to death a twenty-year-old Mexican named Antonio Rodríguez because he had allegedly murdered a woman in town despite no evidence. In response to the execution, Mexican periodicals featured articles denouncing Americans for their violence and inhumanity. A throng of Mexicans protested in the offices of the American-owned *Mexican Herald* while chanting "Remember Antonio Rodríguez" while others chanted "Down with the *gringos*."[13] A few days later, another crowd attacked a group of prominent Americans, and then tore down a US flag and trampled upon it. They lobbed rocks at American schoolchildren, badly hurting one. The rioters gathered steam as they ransacked the offices and homes of Americans. Elsewhere, protesters beat American employees and mandated that musicians not play American music. Mexicans called for boycotts of American products. "The Rodríguez incident demonstrated the mutual antagonisms which made both Mexican and American mobs potentially dangerous…it set the tone of Mexican sentiment which pervaded the years of revolutionary struggle," writes Professor Frederick C. Turner of the University of Connecticut.[14]

Between 1910 and 1920, between 550 and 785 Americans were killed by Mexicans, according to two different US reports.[15] "I have yet to meet a Mexican who has any love for the people of the United States as a whole. There are cases where individual Mexicans have a real affection for individual Americans, but even such cases are

Friendship Circle in San Diego during the Fandango Fronterizo

not common," wrote an American consul stationed in Durango, Mexico, and who estimated that 95 percent of people in his district held anti-American views.[16] In another episode, a Mexican judge sentenced an American to jail for ten years for loaning someone a gun that became a murder weapon.[17] Mexican singers, authors, and playwrights created works that portrayed America in an unflattering light. A singer crooned, "The *gringo* is very despicable, and our eternal enemy."[18] One play featured Uncle Sam grasping at Mexican territory. Political cartoonists caricatured Americans as greedy, portly, loathsome imperialists. Because of this poisonous climate, American expatriates returned home in droves.

After the fall of Díaz in 1911, which precipitated the revolution, an affluent property owner, Francisco Madero, was elected president of Mexico. His governmental reforms were glacial, and his inability to bring about a more lasting peace concerned US officials. Any violent outbreak would threaten to jeopardize US business interests and activities in Mexico. According to one estimate, American companies owned 27 percent of Mexico's land by 1910.[19] During the administration of President William Howard Taft, the US sent troops to the borderlands to project power in the region, and to send the message that they would protect American interests in Mexico.

Many Mexicans didn't want America meddling in their own internal affairs. They interpreted the heightened American military presence as an indication that the US would invade or take over more of Mexico's territories. Mexicans told the American owner of a local hotel that if the US intervened, they would kill her. But young Americans signed up eagerly for Madero's army and comprised the "Foreign Legion," thinking that they were fighting on the side of freedom and liberty. Because of their aptitude, many American and other foreigners became senior military officers, which embittered their Mexican underlings. Madero became tainted with his association with Americans, as his detractors claimed that he was a puppet controlled by American diplomats and bankers. Wanting to push back against this image, Madero implemented several anti-American measures like banning them from working on the railroads.

Meanwhile, instability and volatility were increasing: Rebel forces lead by Félix Díaz battled against General Victoriano Huerta. Hoping to prevent an escalated conflict, the US ambassador to Mexico, Henry Lane Wilson, met in his office with Díaz and Huerta, where they agreed to the "Pact of the Embassy," in which Huerta would betray Madero and stage a coup.

In what became known as *La Decena Trágica* or the Ten Tragic Days, the plan was executed, Huerta became president, and Madero was later assassinated in February 1913. A country that prides itself on democratic values, the US had circumvented a Mexican election and installed a military strongman.

When Woodrow Wilson became president in March 1913, he withheld recognition of Huerta's government. Huerta was clearly in charge and enjoyed support among people, as many lined the streets as he took part in a parade in Mexico City. He even reached a peace accord with rebels in northern Mexico, but he desired US recognition, which would give him more legitimacy and resources to strengthen his power at home. Yet Wilson decided against recognizing Huerta and denounced his administration as a "government of butchers," because it had come to power after a bloody coup.[20] The US even succeeded in getting Great Britain to withdraw its support of Huerta.[21]

Paradoxically, US non-recognition boosted Huerta's popularity at home. The *gringo* imperialists didn't approve of Mexico's government, and the anti-Americanism in Mexico continued unabated. Americans living in Mexico nixed their Fourth of July celebrations and took cover from protesters.[22] Huerta leveraged the xenophobia into boosting his military ranks, as military officials distributed fliers encouraging Mexicans to sign up because the "enemy attack has already begun."[23] One leaflet making the rounds called for the slaughter of all Americans living in Mexico.

Wilson gathered that if he wanted to change Mexico's regime, America would have to play a more active role. Hoping to slow the number of weapons that Huerta was receiving from Europe, Wilson authorized the invasion of the Port of Veracruz in 1914 by eight hundred US Navy and Marine forces. The Americans encountered

The US flag on the border wall in Tijuana

resistance from Mexican forces and also civilians like masons who threw bricks at them. All told, twenty-two Americans and hundreds of Mexicans lost their lives. The US occupation lasted about seven months, which prevented Huerta from obtaining the weaponry needed to successfully fend off his opponents. Huerta eventually left office but the violent struggle for power in Mexico resumed and continued to threaten US interests.

"What the intervention did achieve was the renewal of rancor among Mexicans. Thousands of Veracruzans went quietly into internal exile, avoiding any cooperation with the invaders…Mexican nationalism underwent a surge—with profound and long-lasting consequences," writes Enrique Krauze, a historian.[24] The invasion further validated the anxieties and fears of Mexicans of the *gringo* imperialists, and the clouds of suspicion remained.

Fearing the Bad Hombre

Xenophobia or anti-Mexicanism has also been a trenchant force in American society. For example, the "Juan Crow" era during the twentieth century in which Mexicans were segregated into attending different schools from those of white Americans. Yet in the 1970s, whites in Houston tried to classify Mexicans as white, so Mexican children would have to integrate with black schoolchildren instead of the actual white population. "Now that their 'whiteness' was being used to circumvent desegregation, however, many of them rejected this racial identity," writes Guadalupe San Miguel Jr. in *Brown, Not White*.[25]

This xenophobia toward Mexicans goes back even longer. In the nineteenth century, when the US annexed large swaths of Mexican land, it inherited Mexican nationals who were wary of the new authorities. And many Americans were just as dubious. In his opposition to the Mexican-American War, one congressman noted, "New Mexico…California…are inhabited by a mixed population… incapable of sympathy or assimilation with our own…unprepared to appreciate, sustain, or enjoy, free institutions."[26] That Mexicans could comport with American ideas and values was a bridge too far to accept. After all, Mexicans were the "other" who differed from Americans in race, religion, language, cultures, and traditions.

At the beginning of the twentieth century, Mexicans were migrating in greater numbers to work agricultural jobs for low wages across the South. Taking notice of the increased presence of Mexicans, in 1909 the *New Orleans Times-Picayune* described them as "unambitious, listless, physically weak, irregular, and indolent."[27] It's during this time period, roughly the same years of the Mexican Revolution, that marked one of the most violent and murderous periods in US-Mexican history.

With Mexico undergoing a tumultuous time of conflict, combat, and clashes, there was a power vacuum, especially in the borderlands, which local bandits and vigilantes sought to fill. The lawlessness of the "Wild West" raised concerns not only for Americans living in this region but for US industrialists and diplomats who wanted to protect their assets and interests. But the steady stream of Mexican nationals crossing the border, coupled with Americans struggling and even competing with these unfamiliar people, provoked a veritable panic among Americans who felt that Mexicans were criminals plotting to reclaim long-lost Mexican territories. In 1915, a Georgia newspaper, *Columbus Enquirer-Sun*, ran a story called "Negroes and Mexicans Want

Republic in Tex."[28] An Oklahoma publication claimed Mexicans were planning to kill all Americans in border towns. These stories were exaggerations, but there were cases of Mexicans who raised suspicion and provoked fear. For instance, Basilio Ramos Jr., a Mexican vigilante, came to the US with a pamphlet that listed anti-American ideas that he hoped would help stir up a rebellion, but his plot was discovered when Mexicans turned him in to local security officials. The panic grew when General Frederick Funston, sent by President Wilson to the borderlands, claimed that thousands of Mexican Americans had vowed to support an insurrection organization that would weaken the US, a claim with little if any substantiation.[29]

Left unchecked, these rumors fueled xenophobic panic, which incited American vigilantes to begin raiding the homes of Mexican Americans for firearms and other weapons. They even shot and killed

Peering through the border wall

some of these Mexican Americans for refusing to be arrested and detained. In one tragic episode in 1915, the bodies of thirty Mexican Americans were found in southern Texas, the ghastly consequence of marauding vigilantes, triggered by fear, who took justice into their own hands.

Such extralegal justice was a common occurrence in the region: The Rodríguez lynching wasn't an isolated incident. In June 1911, an angry mob seized Antonio Gómez, a fourteen-year-old Mexican who had been accused of murder, from a Texas prison, and they hanged him from a telephone pole. Even the Americans were unsettled that a child had been tortured and killed, yet the local newspaper was resigned to the fact that justice for the murderers was unlikely to be served: "While indignation is high it is a ten to one shot nothing is ever done to them."[30] Mexican government officials pressed their American counterparts, and local authorities arrested four suspects for the lynching, but they were all found not guilty.[31] That Mexico was able to get US officials to take some action was an important step toward mutual cooperation. But because of the frequent turnover in political regimes during the revolutionary years, it was difficult for Mexican authorities to build and maintain relationships with their American counterparts. The chaos in the political ranks likely inhibited Mexico from seeking and achieving more justice for the wrongs suffered by their citizens at the hands of American vigilantes.

In yet another tragic incident, in 1919 a group of vigilantes captured two Mexican inmates in a Colorado prison who were accused of murdering a police officer. The thugs established a ruse by calling in news of a fake riot so that the police would investigate, leaving the jail relatively unguarded. They loaded the Mexicans into cars and then hanged them from a bridge. Though these outlaws were never apprehended, an investigation found that the Mexicans were innocent of the crimes for which they had been charged.

In *Forgotten Dead*, history professors William Carrigan and Clive Webb document at least 547 Mexicans who were lynched between 1848 and 1928. The entry for Rodríguez reads: "Seized from jail, tied to a tree, and burned alive."[32] The record for Gómez says: "Beaten and dragged behind buggy through the streets by a mob estimated 100." And the listing for the two Mexicans killed in Colorado reads: "Hanged by mob of 100 persons for murder of policeman." Surely there were innumerable, likely thousands, more Mexicans that were killed, but the official documentation is scant and incomplete. For example, the Tuskegee Institute, which tracked lynchings, segments victims into two categories, whites and blacks. It's hard to know how many Mexicans were misidentified in these records. But what is accepted is that public lynchings of Mexicans took place over eighty years, and were roughly concentrated during three periods: (1) the Gold Rush of the 1850s, when Mexican migrants worked as laborers amid declining yields, which created an atmosphere of uneasiness and anxiety; (2) the American Reconstruction Years of 1870s, when African Americans moved north and Mexicans took up agricultural jobs in the American South and Southwest; and (3) the Mexican Revolution, from 1910 to 1920, when violent outbreaks threatened the safety and security of the borderlands.[33]

Indeed, Americans found themselves strangers in their own lands that they had obtained through acquisition or conquest. Intrepid settlers moved to the borderlands for a chance of striking it big for their families back home. But they encountered Mexicans in higher numbers, and they couldn't communicate readily with them, nor were they as knowledgeable about the geography and terrain. Life in these parts was tough. Carrigan and Webb explain the motivations for their gruesome acts:

> Under such conditions and as the inheritors of a tradition of vigilantism...it is hardly surprising that Anglos allowed their frustrations to explode into mob violence. These frustrations...were rarely cited by the perpetrators...Instead lynchers consistently defended their actions as rational responses to the ineffectual state of the frontier courts.[34]

While it's factual that courts in Texas and California were overworked, the impulses for such outrageous and murderous behavior rest upon fear, anxiety, and hate. This is a bloody chapter in American history that has until recently not been explored comprehensively by scholars. With little doubt, Carrigan and Webb conclude that "racial prejudice was the primary force in fomenting mob violence against Mexicans."[35]

As evidenced by the Americans killing Mexicans or vice versa, US-Mexican relations have a gory, gruesome past. This specter of violence has cast a long shadow, and the suspicions and doubts on both sides remain. When US and Mexican political figures begin demonizing one another, they are ripping the scabs off wounds that have formed over many decades.

Yet while history has left several scars, these two neighboring countries have managed to work together, and even forge a close alliance, despite the odds. Indeed, we can build a stronger relationship, one based on facts.

Border Patrol agents during the Fandango Fronterizo festival in 2017

Nicolas Rodriguez-Brizuela, Douglas Brinkley, Kabir Sehgal, Arturo O'Farrill at the border wall

Chapter 5

THE WALLS CAME TUMBLING DOWN
The true nature of migration and jobs

"The main reason for my return is family. I could help
them while I was there, but family comes before money."[1]
—JOSÉ ARELLANO CORREA, taxi driver in Mexico

"If we do not create additional jobs in Mexico, Mexicans will merely
walk across the border looking for jobs in the north. We want to export
goods, not people. Our intention with NAFTA is to create additional
jobs and make wages grow, not to steal jobs from the US."[2]
—CARLOS SALINAS DE GORTARI, president of Mexico

"...because NAFTA means jobs, American jobs and
good-paying American jobs. If I didn't believe that,
I wouldn't support this agreement."[3]
—BILL CLINTON, 42nd president of the United States

Our goal is to tear down the mental wall between Americans and
Mexicans. Given the charged and conflicted history, this is a tall
order. But when the prevailing political rhetoric becomes overrun with
invectives and insults, it falls upon citizens to remind and reawaken
one another about the true nature of our relationship: Nearly a million
Americans live in Mexico, and millions more Mexicans live in the
US. We aren't just neighbors but one another's brothers and sisters,
madres y padres, nephews and nieces, *tíos y tías*. We are *familia*.

We're also co-founders, colleagues, coworkers, collaborators, counterparties, customers, and clients. Mexico is America's third-largest trading partner. Both nations represent vital sources of income and jobs for each other. The cement in your office-building parking lot might come from CEMEX, a Mexican cement producer, which has hundreds of facilities throughout the US. The bread in your pantry may come from Bimbo, a Mexican firm that is the largest bakery in the US. Similarly, Mexicans drink Coca-Cola and Starbucks coffee, and they use Facebook and Twitter to connect with friends.

The sheer volume of people, goods, and services that move across the border reveals a robust and reliable partnership that arguably makes both countries stronger. This isn't the Mexico that you hear about on the evening news or in the trending tweetstorm. But when you focus on the facts, evidence of a vibrant collaboration emerges.

How are Hispanics affecting US demographics?

Hispanics are the largest ethnic group in America, with 58 million in 2016, which accounts for 18 percent of the overall population. This is a material increase of over 500 percent, from the 9.6 million that resided in the US in 1970. This multi-decade surge is responsible for 50 percent of America's population growth since the beginning of the twenty-first century.[4] As baby boomers retire and exit the workforce in greater numbers, Hispanics are increasingly filling the job ranks. Hispanics are also the youngest ethnic group, with a median age of 28, compared with 43 for whites and 34 for blacks.[5] And they accounted for roughly 11 percent of the electorate in 2016.[6]

Antonio Sanchez plays the drums during the recording sessions

The US Census Bureau projects that the Hispanic population will grow to 119 million by 2060, making up about 28 percent of the total American population.[7] Sooner than that, in 2045, the white population will fall to less than half, which means it will be the largest minority group in the US. This trend is happening more quickly among those who are under eighteen: By 2020, whites in this cohort will be outnumbered by other minorities. "Minorities will be the source of all of the growth in the nation's youth and working age population, most of the growth in its voters, and much of the growth in its consumers and tax base as far into the future as we can see," according to a Brookings Institution report.[8] Already, Hispanics outnumber whites in California and are the largest ethnic group at 39 percent of the population.[9]

If demography really is destiny, then America's future will be progressively shaped by Hispanics, which may alter immigration and labor laws, in addition to US foreign policy toward Latin American countries such as Mexico. Not to mention, US culinary preferences have changed, as salsa has outpaced ketchup as the highest selling condiment in America.[10] As Hispanics gain in prominence, whites, and other racial and ethnic groups, may feel anxious about their place in society, and struggle with how to cope with waning influence. With these tectonic shifts in demographics, there will be more need for artists and activists to help expand empathy, by creating works that stimulate discussion and habituate people to come to terms with these new cultural dynamics. For starters, companies can institute training programs that help people become more aware of their unconscious biases, like what Starbucks did in spring 2018. It closed all of its stores in the US to ensure that its 175,000 employees received instruction on how to listen and learn from those who are different. Another idea would be for cultural institutions to program more artists who come from Latin American traditions. Even US and Mexican governmental institutions can promote cross-border cultural exchange and encourage tourists to visit both countries. Perhaps airlines can put albums on in-flight entertainment systems that include the music of different nations, and then display these albums as default listening choices.

How many Mexicans are in the US?

The word *Hispanic* is a catch-all term that refers to those from Spanish-speaking countries in Latin America. Mexicans constituted 63 percent of Hispanics in the US or 36 million people in 2015 (followed by the next largest group, Puerto Ricans, at 5.3 million).[11] Mexicans have always been the largest group, but the diversification of the Hispanic community has also increased. That is, the Mexican share of the total Hispanic population has declined from a peak of 81 percent in 1860, when there were just 155,000 Hispanics living in the US.

To be clear, the 36 million Mexicans include 24.3 million who were born in the US and 11.7 million who were born in Mexico in 2014.[12] That means that they account for 42 percent of America's foreign-born population. Of those who were born in Mexico, 64 percent live in California, Texas, and Illinois. They're also younger, with a median age of 41, than the overall foreign-born average of 44. The vast majority of these Mexicans, 80 percent, are of working age and take part in America's workforce in higher rates than the average for all foreign-born people. Foreign-born Mexicans work across several sectors in the US such as construction and transportation. They typically work in low-skill jobs as low-wage workers.[13] Thus they don't make as much money, with a median family income of $37,390 per year, versus $49,487, the average for foreign-born households in 2014. Almost 30 percent of foreign-born Mexicans live in poverty, which is also higher than the foreign-born average, and 47 percent lack healthcare insurance. Only 6 percent have a college degree, which is far less than the 29 percent of everyone else who was born abroad, and about 70 percent of these Mexicans aren't fluent in English, which is higher than the foreign-born average of 50 percent.[14] In sum, Mexicans comprise the biggest pool of foreign-born people in the US, work at higher rates in the labor force, and earn less money.

But the rate of Mexicans migrating to the US has slowed and even reversed in recent years. Between 2009 and 2014, an estimated

Mandy Gonzales sings at Power Station studio in June 2018

one million Mexicans returned to Mexico, whereas 870,000 arrived, which amounted to a *net loss* of 130,000. "This is something that we've seen coming. It's been almost ten years that migration from Mexico has really slowed down," says Mark Hugo, head of Hispanic research at Pew.[15] Many Mexicans cited wanting to return home to their families as a top reason. This phenomenon may also be driven by fewer jobs and economic opportunities, as the US was still suffering the aftereffects of the Great Recession of 2008 or because there were more economic opportunities in Mexico, as its economy has grown moderately since the financial crisis. In addition, the US government has taken tougher actions toward foreign-born people: Congress furnished $18 billion in 2012 for security measures involving immigration, which was 24 percent more than the budget of the FBI, DEA, and other law enforcement agencies put together.[16] This enabled the government to add more border patrol agents to its ranks and increase security measures at the border, among other measures. By 2016, President Barack Obama was derisively known among immigration-rights advocates as the "Deporter in Chief" because his administration deported 2.5 million people, which was more than previous presidents.[17] This happened in part because there was more congressional funding. Also, Obama's administration ramped up efforts to deport those who had immediately crossed the border such as gang members and those convicted of crimes.[18] Yet despite his track record, he didn't preside over any large additions to the border wall.

It's important to note that the US has long relied upon Mexicans to fill jobs, and it has even created authorized programs to facilitate the movement of migrant workers. During World War II, the US experienced a labor shortage, so the government created the "Bracero Program" (*bracero* means "laborer" in Spanish) in 1942 that ran until 1964. The program brought in 4.6 million migrant workers, many of whom stayed and became permanent residents. After the program ended, the US implemented more restrictive measures that limited the flow of Mexican migrants. But after letting millions of Mexicans in, it was difficult to reverse course in practice so dramatically: From 1965 to 1986, 80 percent of the 5.7 million Mexican migrants were unauthorized.[19] Therefore, another reason for the recent decline in Mexican-born people in the US is that it's being compared to the post-Bracero wave of migration.

How many undocumented people are there in the US?

All told, there were about 11 million undocumented people of any ethnicity in the US in 2016, which has decreased by 9.8 percent since 2007. These 11 million people make up about 3.4 percent of America's total population.[20]

Of the 11.7 million Mexicans who live in the US, about 50 percent or 5.6 million were undocumented in 2016. But the population of undocumented Mexicans has dropped 19 percent, from 6.9 million in 2007. Even though the number of Mexicans has declined, they still comprise about half of the unauthorized population in America, but they don't make up an obvious majority. That is, the number of undocumented people from other countries has increased from 5 million in 2009 to 5.4 million in 2014, a boost of 8 percent.[21] Many of these people come from other Latin American as well as Asian and African countries. Some 60 percent of undocumented people have lived in the US for more than a decade, so they have long and familial ties with Americans.[22]

How many undocumented Mexicans cross the border?

It's difficult to pinpoint the exact number of unauthorized crossings. The border receives a heavy amount of traffic, with 350 million people crossing it legally each year.[23] But the DHS estimates that the number of successful unauthorized crossings from Mexico has decreased from 1.7 million in 2005 to 170,000 in 2015, a decline of 90 percent.[24] Most of the unauthorized crossings happen in southern Texas, in the area near the Rio Grande River.[25]

Yet overall, the number of Mexican apprehensions has dropped markedly, from 1.6 million in 2000 to 192,969 in 2016, a decline of 88 percent. This most recent number was less than the 222,847 apprehensions of non-Mexicans at US borders.[26] In 2017, the number of apprehensions for unauthorized border crossing dropped to the lowest since 1971. "Overall, removals are down because the border's under better control than it has been in forty-five years," said Tom Homan, an official at Immigration and Customs Enforcement.[27] The reasons for the drop-off in unauthorized Mexican crossings range from enhanced border security to more economic opportunities in Mexico.

Do Mexicans bring drugs?

Yes, some do. All told, the Customs and Border Patrol (CBP) confiscated 246,000 kilograms of drugs at border crossings in the Southwest versus almost 600,000 kilograms in other areas in 2016.[28] The same year in San Diego alone, US authorities seized 83,000 kilograms of drugs such as marijuana, heroin, and cocaine that came via Mexico.[29] But finding these drugs is like looking for a needle in a haystack. Much of the drugs don't come through the border wall but concealed in cars, trucks, ships, planes, drones, or even via underground tunnels and catapults. In many cases, vehicles that are carrying legitimate goods like fruits and vegetables have secret compartments with drugs that make it incredibly difficult to detect, as 23 million passenger cars go through the Tijuana–San Diego crossing each year. "If you put up one wall, they find a way around it," says an official at the DHS.[30] There have been approximately 224 tunnels discovered since 1990 along the border, even some with elevators and lighting.[31] "The wall won't stop the flow of drugs into the United States," says a fellow at the Brookings Institution, who also points out the numerous other ways drugs enter the country.[32] According to the DEA, 95 percent of drugs come to the US via containers on boats.[33]

But just as the drugs flow south to north, the money and weapons move from north to south. Mexican drug cartels make about $19 to $29 billion from sales in the US.[34] The money that these cartels make enables them to maintain sophisticated and professional operations, which employ tens of thousands of people. "I wish I had a unit dedicated to checking vehicles going south for guns and money," said a CBP officer.[35] About $300 million has been confiscated at checkpoints from those traveling south into Mexico. As for guns, about 70 percent or 73,684 of those confiscated in Mexico, from 2009 to 2014, originated in the US.[36] Drug violence has killed 80,000 in Mexico, with at least 32,000 missing, since the Mexican War on Drugs began in 2006.[37] The murder rate in Mexico has spiked from under 10 in 2007 to 18.7 per 100,000 people in 2016, and gun violence has had a devastating effect on families and neighborhoods across Mexico.[38]

The interconnectedness of drugs, money, and guns makes up a vicious circle that threatens the health, safety, and security of those on both sides of the border. In the US, there is a voracious appetite for drugs, with 27 million Americans over the age of 12, roughly 10 percent of the total population, who used illicit drugs in 2015.[39] In one jarring comparison, 62,497 Americans died from drug overdoses in 2015, more than those who perished during the entire Vietnam War.[40] This insatiable demand for drugs in the US and resilient supply from Mexico are tangled and twisted forces that can be felt in major metropolises and rural communities in both countries.

Do Mexicans bring crime?

Immigrants, Mexicans included, don't commit crime in higher rates than the native-born population, according to several studies. Foreign-born young men are incarcerated at one-fourth the rate as that of the native-born population: "Young native-born men are much more likely to commit crimes than comparable foreign-born men. This disparity also holds for young men likely to be undocumented immigrants: Mexicans, Salvadoran, and Guatemalan men," concludes the National Academy of Sciences.[41] In fact, first-generation immigrants, those who were the first in their families born in the US, are actually 50 percent less likely to commit crimes than subsequent generations. The same study found that "immigration *inversely* relates to crime rates; that is, the more immigrants in the area, the lower the crime rate tends to be."[42]

According to a CATO Institute study in 2017: "Illegal immigrants are 44 percent less likely to be incarcerated than natives."[43] Of the 11 million undocumented individuals, some 820,000 or 7 percent were convicted of a crime, and 2.7 percent have been convicted of a felony.[44] Even in California, where there is a large immigrant population, native-born men are incarcerated at a 2.5 times higher rate than those born elsewhere.[45] "Immigrants in general—unauthorized immigrants in particular—are a self-selected group who generally come to the US to work…most of them want to keep their nose down and do their business, and they're sensitive to the fact that they're vulnerable," says Marc Rosenblum, who works at a nonpartisan immigration organization.[46] *The Economist* even calls crime among immigrants a "non-problem."[47]

A landmark study among several universities examined immigration and crime rates in 200 cities over many decades: It found that in 70 percent of these areas, as immigrant populations increased, crime either remained stable or declined. The upshot is that immigration may actually reduce crime, or maybe there is no relation between immigration and crime at all.[48] These findings are surely inconvenient to those who espouse the theory that undocumented people are stirring up trouble in American communities.

Of course, there are incidents of undocumented Mexicans involved in crime, some of which are gang and drug related. Heroic American men and women who protect our border have also lost their lives in the line of duty, as have Mexican border officials.[49] Some 55,000 undocumented individuals were in federal prisons in 2010, and about 300,000 were in state and local prisons. The majority of these were Mexicans, according to the Government Accountability Office.[50] Of course, there are bad apples in every country. But there doesn't appear to be a causal link between immigration and crime, at least not according to peer-reviewed research and academic journals.

Will the wall stop undocumented Mexicans from entering the US?

No. Undocumented persons don't just come by foot. They come to the US via cars, trucks, trains, boats, and planes. In many cases, they travel on legal visas and stay after the expiration date. By 2012,

58 percent of the total undocumented population had overstayed their visas.[51] In 2016, some 416,500 people had overstayed their visas.[52] It would be more effective to implement policies that curb those who overstay their visas, and to introduce a comprehensive e-verification program that requires employers to hire only US citizens, than to invest billions in a border wall that people can fly over in a plane.

Admittedly, building a wall might serve as a deterrent to those from Central and Latin America who want to cross the border. It may also slow crossings. After the border wall was built near San Diego in the 1990s, the number of apprehensions decreased markedly. As a result, the number of border crossings went up in areas where there were fewer barriers. But crediting the border wall as the single determining factor for reduced apprehensions is too simplistic. The increased presence of border agents and sophisticated surveillance technology has helped to slow the overall number of attempted crossings.[53] Yet stopping entirely the flow of people across a nearly 2,000-mile border is impossible. Even the conservative Heritage Foundation notes in an essay titled "The Wall Is Not Enough"[54] that there should be funding for technologies that detect those who cross the border without proper documentation.

An enhanced wall might even have unintended consequences. Mexican smugglers will be able to charge more for crossings, which will concentrate additional money in the hands of these professional traffickers. One smuggler even thanked Trump because he believes the wall is a giant distraction: "This is never going to stop, neither the narcotrafficking nor the illegals. There will be more tunnels. More holes. If it doesn't go over, it will go under."[55] The smugglers will inevitably figure out more advanced methods for getting people and drugs across the border. What is more, a concrete wall might hinder border agents who won't be able to anticipate or detect border crossings: "Seeing through a fence allows agents to anticipate and mobilize, prior to illegal immigrants actually climbing or cutting through the fence," observed one agent.[56]

No matter the technology, a wall can't stop everyone. The catalysts that make people attempt crossings range from people desiring better jobs to simply wanting to be with their families. Any plan that is intended to slow or stop the number of unauthorized crossings must also address the reasons why people migrate in the first place. For example, if there were better economic opportunities in Mexico, then more might stay in their home country rather than risk their lives to pass through the rugged borderlands.

But as a symbol, the wall sends the message "stay out," and it's this mentality of xenophobia that may be seeping into the body politic of both nations. As we're seeing, even the *intent* to enhance the wall has reawakened suspicions of Americans that Mexicans are criminals, and for Mexicans, that Americans are arrogant *gringos*. We've been here many times before.

Performing at the border wall in 2018

Will Mexico pay for the wall?

No.[57]

Are undocumented Mexicans stealing American jobs?

Not exactly. The National Academy of Sciences, Engineering, and Medicine finds that immigration doesn't negatively impact the overall employment levels of Americans.[58]

Certainly, undocumented Mexicans fill low-skilled job openings in the US. But these jobs are not desirable to native-born Americans with similar skill levels. These occupations are often physically intense and unpleasant—like working fourteen hours a day, six days a week, and earning $11,000 per year, with no benefits.[59]

For instance, the Georgia governor introduced a program that replaced migrant agricultural workers with probationers. After a short while on the job, many convicts quit: "Those guys out here weren't out there thirty minutes and they got the bucket and just threw them in the air and say, 'Bonk this. I ain't with this. I can't do this.' They just left, took off across the field walking," said one parolee.[60] "If you remove Mexican labor, farms would go out of business. That's a given," said a dairy farmer in Wisconsin.[61]

According to one study, the professions that have the greatest number of immigrants who haven't graduated high school include cooks, agricultural workers, and maids. Native-born individuals with the same education level tend to be truck drivers, cashiers, and custodians.[62] Native-born but low-skilled Americans have advantages of legal status, certain knowledge of the local job market and culture, established networks, and fluency in English that present them with a different set of job opportunities.

The same study indicates that low-skilled immigrant and native labor are not really competing in the same spheres, and with educational attainment increasing in the US, the pool of native-born workers with less than a high school education will shrink further. The US will need a pool of unskilled workers from somewhere, because according to the Bureau of Labor Statistics, by 2022 there will be 4 million more jobs that do not require a high school degree. About 16 percent of the US labor force is foreign-born, which is important because baby boomers are retiring in greater numbers. Without the immigrants, the workforce would contract and economic growth would decline: "We need these workers not just to fill jobs but to increase productivity, which has diminished sharply," writes Vanda Felbab-Brown of the Brookings Institution.[63]

Besides, American workers have more to fear from automation, which could remove 73 million American jobs by 2030, according to McKinsey, an international consultancy.[64] From self-driving cars to automated legal services, both blue- and white-collar professions will undergo seismic changes in both countries in the coming years.

What are the economic effects of NAFTA?

In 1994, the North American Free Trade Agreement (NAFTA) replaced the Canada–United States Free Trade Agreement, including Mexico with the goal of eliminating trade and investment barriers among the three nations. At the time of its passing, NAFTA enjoyed bipartisan support. President George H. W. Bush negotiated much of the terms, and President Bill Clinton signed the deal.

The agreement was unusual among modern trade agreements because two of the countries were wealthy, and one was a low-income developing economy.[65] By intertwining Mexico's economy with those of the US and Canada, some supporters believed that there would be more growth in economic opportunities in Mexico, which would limit the number of immigrants leaving the country. In other words, NAFTA was implemented, in part, to curb undocumented immigration. Amid the debate of the agreement, economist Paul Krugman observed, "For the United States, NAFTA is essentially a foreign policy rather than economic issue."[66]

At the time, Mexico's inclusion generated much debate about potential job losses in the developed economies and the prospect of a "race to the bottom" in terms of environmental and labor conditions. Side agreements were negotiated in 1993 to settle environmental, labor, and agricultural issues. And these terms were steadily introduced through 2008.[67] NAFTA's implementation ushered in an era of reduced tariffs on US and Mexican goods. The average tariff rate applied by the US to imports from Mexico declined from 3.15 percent in 1993 to 0.52 percent in 2001.

Since NAFTA, regional trade among the US, Mexico, and Canada grew rapidly from about $290 billion in 1993 to more than $1.1 trillion in 2016.[68] US exports to Mexico grew at an average annual rate of about 8.1 percent from 1993 to 2016, outpacing the average annual nominal GDP growth rate of 4.5 percent over this period. US imports from Mexico grew at a faster average annual rate of 9.8 percent. Yet the size of Mexican imports as a share of the US economy is small: just 1.6 percent versus 0.6 percent before NAFTA.[69] Put another way, economists estimate that NAFTA has modestly boosted the US GDP by 0.5 percent or $80 billion.[70] That's a "drop in the bucket," said Beth Ann Bovino, US economist at S&P, when you factor in the overall size of the American economy.[71]

Mexico has indeed benefitted from a closer economic relationship with America. The US foreign direct investment in Mexico has swelled over 560 percent, from $15 billion to $100 billion. Perhaps most telling is that after the financial crisis of 2008, its economy bounced back within a couple years. Had there been a protracted recession in Mexico, there may have been a greater number of undocumented persons entering the US.

But NAFTA hasn't been entirely rosy for Mexico. In America, the press focuses on the increase in auto manufacturing jobs in Mexico. Less known is that Mexico has lost an estimated two million jobs in agriculture, as Mexican farmers compete with American farm goods, which are heavily subsidized by the US government, like corn. "The upshot is you have a country that was practically self-sufficient in corn, its staple food crops, [that] is now highly dependent on imports to feed itself," says Laura Carlsen, an academic based in Mexico City.[72] Economists contend that NAFTA has also exacerbated inequality between the more highly developed northern states and the agrarian south.[73]

There are drawbacks in the US too, and critics blame NAFTA for having contributed to economic inequality, the loss of manufacturing jobs, wage stagnation, and yawning trade deficits. US companies have moved factories to Mexico to take advantage of lower labor costs, which has cost American jobs. One estimate shows that 600,000 American jobs may have been lost because of NAFTA, and another study indicates that 15,000 jobs are lost every year.[74] Other economists contend that it's America's trade relationship with China, not Mexico, that is responsible for many of these losses. Yet when you look at total export-related jobs, America may have gained 5 million new jobs in the years since NAFTA went into effect.[75]

On the flip side, lower labor costs can mean cheaper prices, so that more Americans can afford certain goods, and their standard of living is enhanced. The pain induced by NAFTA might be concentrated in highly visible industries, but the benefits appear to be more spread out. For example, Americans buy more than 40 million televisions every year, and 75 percent of them are made in Mexico.[76] If companies manufactured these goods in the US, their costs would go up, and fewer Americans could afford them. Obviously, the complexity of global and regional trade can be difficult to assess, and economists continue to vigorously debate how much NAFTA is responsible for economic outcomes. One 2016 report attempted to summarize the impact of NAFTA, which has led to "a substantial increase in trade volumes…a small increase in US welfare; and little to no change in US aggregate employment."[77]

Is Mexico beating the US economically?

When it comes to trade, winning and losing isn't so cut-and-dried. By almost every economic measure and indicator, the US has a larger, more robust, more diversified, and wealthier economy. Poverty levels in Mexico remain high at around 44 percent of the population, and little has changed since 1994.[78] Mexicans have not experienced a material increase in wages in line with their counterparts in the US during the NAFTA period.[79] Mexico's official unemployment rate has averaged around 4 percent, slightly higher than the 3.1 percent in the pre-NAFTA years of 1990 to 1994.

Some consider the US trade deficit with Mexico as a "loss." Pre-NAFTA, the US had a $1.3 billion surplus with Mexico in 1993, which has turned into a deficit of $64 billion in 2017. But trade isn't war. Rather, it can make countries mutually interdependent, so that it's more profitable to maintain the peace than to provoke conflict. Free trade should reflect the natural supply and demand of goods and services between countries.

Critics like to cite the automobile industry as evidence that America is losing because of NAFTA. Because of the agreement, Mexican automotive products gained access to the US, and over time, auto production was moved to Mexico. Among US imports of motor vehicles and parts, the share from Mexico rose from 11 percent in 1993 to 31 percent by 2016.[80] The US runs a large trade deficit with Mexico in motor vehicles, at $74 billion in 2016. What's more, the number of Americans employed in automotive manufacturing has declined by 348,000 from 1994 to 2013, while Mexico's employment in this sector has quadrupled to 552,000.[81]

Yet the lower labor costs in Mexico keep the production costs low, which make US-branded cars such as Ford and GM more competitive in the global marketplace. The increased profit margins of these companies make the stocks of these companies more attractive to global institutional investors who manage the retirement money for millions of Americans.

Thus working out winners and losers, in the aggregate, is arduous. To be sure, if you're an auto worker in the Midwest who is out of work, NAFTA looks like a negative. But if you buy garments and electronics from Mexico, or your 401(k) retirement savings are invested in companies with operations in Mexico, you might look at NAFTA as a positive.

What happens if NAFTA ends?

If the US withdraws from NAFTA, it would start the clock on a six-month period where NAFTA rules would still be in place. It's likely that negotiations would begin immediately for new bilateral tariff regimes and other rules. Trade wouldn't stop and may not even decline that much, but it would be less efficient given the uncertainty about the new regime and a return to tariffs on at least some goods.

In Mexico, tariffs on (non-NAFTA) imports average about 7 percent for most favored nations according to the World Trade Organization.[82] If this rate were imposed on US goods, Mexican demand for US goods would likely decline given the higher costs. In the US agricultural sector, where Mexico is the third-largest export market, there might be an immediate impact, as there would be more price competition due to higher tariffs. One US farmer estimated that the price of corn for his Mexican customers could rise 15 percent if tariffs revert to pre-NAFTA levels.[83] Among agricultural exports to Mexico, corn was the largest share at $2.6 billion in 2016, followed by soybeans at $1.5 billion.[84]

Dissolving NAFTA would also mark the end to an era of foreign policy cooperation between the US and Mexico, which signaled to the rest of the world that the Mexican state was committed to structural economic reforms and was a player in the global market. Mexico would likely feel the greatest impacts on a macro level if NAFTA were ended, from declines in its currency value and stock market, to a jump in bond yields from investor fears about declining foreign investment, which would hurt growth. Because the peso would likely depreciate, the US trade deficit with Mexico might actually grow.[85]

Moreover, the disbandment of NAFTA may embitter Mexico and push them toward anti-American policies that flout democratic norms. "The country faces two extreme political futures," writes Shannon O'Neil of the Council on Foreign Relations. "It could evolve into a highly developed democracy such as Spain, or it could deteriorate into a weak and unreliable state, dependent on and hostage to a drug economy, an Afghanistan."[86] By shunning Mexico, the US may have to deal with even worse consequences later.

For the US, there would be industry-specific effects, but any changes in trade patterns due to an end of NAFTA would be small in relation to the overall size of the US economy. Yet prices will likely go up: "It's difficult to see the economic benefits of increasing prices on Mexican and Canadian imports for 45 million low-income Americans (as well as everyone else) in an effort to save just some of the jobs in an [auto] industry that accounts for roughly 85 of every 1,000 full-time jobs in the US labor force," according to S&P.[87]

What's more, it's unlikely that manufacturing jobs will return to the US, as companies can still assemble cars and make garments in other countries with cheaper labor costs.

Obviously, it's difficult to isolate the effects of NAFTA because there are so many other factors that drive economic activity such as global trade patterns, interest rates, government spending, and taxes.

When you look past the hyperbolic news cycle, it becomes clear that the relationship between the US and Mexico is complex and far ranging. Thus, to present any one solution as a panacea, like an enhanced border wall, is too simplistic.

Given the intertwined nature of the US and Mexican economies, Americans and Mexicans should root for one another. If Mexico's economy fails, there will be more undocumented immigrants coming to the US. If the American economy suffers, less investment will pour into the parts of Mexico's economy that need it most. The destinies of our nations are, in part, dependent on each other.

A wall doesn't represent the good-faith coexistence of our nations. But an international park or trans-border *fandango* speaks to the shared responsibility of the border. Putting aside the negativity and political rancor, what becomes apparent is that Mexicans and Americans are driven by similar things: providing for their families, finding meaningful work, and prospering into the future.

Music can certainly unleash our better angels and inspire more to find commonality with each other. When we replace the image of the wall with that of the *fandango*, we see those across the border for who they truly are.

Luis Villalobos and Alberto Villalobos look for their brother Ernesto Villalobos on the other side of the wall at the Fandango Fronterizo festival in 2018

Luis Villalobos plays at the wall during the Fandango Fronterizo in 2018

AFTERWORD
by Ambassador Andrew Young

When I was in the midst of the civil rights movement, I knew that we could only change so many minds with facts and figures. It's hard to get someone who is stuck in their ways to alter their opinion or perspective. You can't fight fire with fire. You have to turn the temperature down and let things simmer, so that you can create space to listen to each other, and most importantly, to grow.

In order to dramatize our perspective, we created public spectacles so that more people would notice. For example, we would time our marches so that they would make the evening news, and more folks could be awakened to the inhumane treatment of those who believed in oppressed ideologies. That was part of the brilliance of Dr. Martin Luther King Jr. He had a knack for timing. He knew when to raise his voice and when to keep calm. He could read a crowd and then before you know it, they were nodding their "amens" and "hallelujahs."

Dr. King also understood the power of arts and culture. He knew that music could speak to the heart and bring about feelings of passion, excitement, and healing. He forged a friendship with gospel singer Mahalia Jackson. One of the most public civil rights activists was singer Harry Belafonte. There has always been a nexus of politics and music, and we should welcome the people and projects that blur these lines because they make us think about issues in unexpected ways.

Fandango at the Wall is a project that mixes music with a message. The debate over the border wall isn't going to be settled with rational facts and figures, because these things are already out there and they aren't convincing those who believe otherwise. Instead, by bringing together people and musicians of all kinds, this project will help more people see and appreciate the shared culture between the US and Mexico.

I must admit that I didn't know much about the intricacies of the Mexican Revolution or the natural habitats that risk being ruined by the building of the border wall. By putting the US-Mexico relationship in a broader and more holistic context, what emerges is a fuller understanding of our neighbor to the south. We're connected and in it together. If one of our countries fails, the other will also suffer the consequences. We have to do what we can to promote success across the border, among the people of both nations.

I am naturally partial to this book because it is authored by my godson, Kabir Sehgal, who has been writing and making music since he was a kid. When he was in second grade, he interviewed me for his school newspaper, and he has always had an industrious spirit. I've often told him to slow down because he is constantly in a hurry to get things done. In partnering with Arturo O'Farrill, he has found a talented companion who plays music with emotion and poignancy. Both Kabir and Arturo have made a sparkling contribution not just to literature and music but to everyone who believes our people and countries can and must do better.

As you take this project to heart, ask yourself: "What border do I want to blur?" When you start thinking like this, you'll be surprised with the walls around you that start to fall.

MUSICAL REPERTOIRE

The recording of the full repertoire is sold and available separately. I submitted this manuscript to the publisher in late-June 2018, so I'm listing all the songs that we recorded below. Yet I'm not 100 percent sure what songs will make it on the album. Arturo and I have heard only a few rough mixes of the music as of this writing. The full and final repertoire, and music production information, will come with the two-CD package, and will also be available online.

Big Band Repertoire

- El Maquech
- Amor Sin Fronteras
- Invisible Suite: Invisible Cities
- Invisible Suite: Free Falling Borderless
- Invisible Suite: Invisible Beings
- Fly Away
- Tabla Rasa
- Somos Sur
- Minotauro
- Jaiicasosebaim Noone
- Up Against the Wall

Small Group Repertoire

- El Pijul
- Xalapa Bang

- Hummingbird Blues
- Cielito Lindo
- Line in the Sand
- Chant
- Birth

Son Jarocho Repertoire

- El Siquisiri
- El Cascabel
- El Cupido
- Julia
- La Bamba
- Guanabana
- La Morena
- El Pájaro Cú
- El Buscapiers
- Las Patronas
- Bemba y Tablao
- Identitadas
- Son de Las Pablenos
- Conga Patria

LYRICS

Lyrics provided by Jorge Francisco Castillo
Translations by Jorge Francisco Castillo

Son Jarocho Songs

These are well-known *son jarocho* songs that are performed at *fandangos*. We recorded them as part of the sessions:

- El Siquisiri
- El Cascabel
- El Cupido
- La Bamba
- Guanabana
- La Morena
- El Pájaro Cú
- El Buscapies
- Bemba y Tablao
- Son de Las Poblanas
- Conga Patria
- Las Patronas

These are songs that aren't traditional *son jarocho* songs that have lyrics and that we recorded:

- Xalapa Bang!
- Amor Sin Fronteras
- Hummingbird Blues
- Line in the Sand

El Siquisiri

The *son* that starts all *fandangos*. It functions like a blessing, salutation, and invitation—for people to join the *fandango*.

Permiso le pido al dia
Para empesar la jornada
Quiera dios que la versada
Tenga valor y poesía
Hermosa perla Maria
Comienzo por saludar
Con la música y el verso
Y aunque el mundo esta disperso
Aquí les vengo a cantar

Translation

I ask the day for permission
To begin this journey
God allows the lyrics
To have courage and poetry
Maria, you are a beautiful pearl

I begin by greeting
With the music and the lyrics
And even though the world is apart
Here I will sing for you

El Cascabel

The title translates as the "rattle" of a rattlesnake.
The lyrics invoke metaphors about the rattlesnake.

Yo soy como el cascabel
Que ante nadie se rebaja
Si alguien testerea mi piel
Le aviso con mi sonaja
Que mi mordedura es cruel

Translation

I am like the rattle snake
That is not afraid of anybody
If someone treats my skin
I let them know with my rattle
That my bite is cruel

El Cupido

A traditional *son* that talks about the cupid and his arrow that connects lovers.

Yo le pregunte a cupido
Remedios para olvidar
Y me contesto afligido
Remedios no puedo dar
De ese mal yo he padecido
Y no he podido sanar
Hay cupido cupido, cupido
Cupido cupido chiquito
Cupido cupido, cupido
Cupido dame un besito

Translation

I asked cupid
Remedies to forget
Afflicted cupid answered
I cannot give you a remedy
I had suffered from that pain
And I have not been able to heal
Cupid cupid cupid
Cupid, cupid, you tiny one
Cupid, cupid, cupid
Cupid, give me a little kiss

La Bamba

A traditional *son* that goes back to the seventeenth century when pirates attacked Veracruz. It became a war anthem when the US troops invaded Veracruz in 1914.

Para subir al cielo se necesita
Una escalera grande y otra chiquita
Hay arriba y arriba y arriba ire
Yo no soy marinero por ti sere
Por ti sere por ti sere

Translation

To climb to heaven
You need
A big ladder and a small one
Up and up and up and up I will go
I am not a sailor, because of you I will be one.
I will be one, I will be one.

Guanabana

A romantic and erotic song based on the name of a fruit (soursop).

La guanabana imperial
Es una fruta sencilla
Hay que saberla chupar
Pa' sacarle la semilla
Guanabana dulce y azucarada
Que chupa que chupa y chupa
Y no saca nada.

Translation

The imperial guanabana
It is a simple fruit
You have to know how to suck
To get the seed out of it
Sweet and sugary guanabana
Who sucks, who sucks and sucks
Who sucks and does not take anything

La Morena

Traditional *son* dedicated to a brunette, or in some cases, to Mother Earth.

Morenita sin tu amor
No tengo quien me consuele
Que no te da compasión
Que yo por ti me desvele
Y este pobre corazón
Por todas partes me duele
Me voy a salir al fresco
Por que la calor me mata
Vida mia, si lo merezco,
Dame una flor de tu mata

Translation

Brunette without your love
I have no one to comfort me
That does not give you compassion
That I for you unveil me

And this poor heart
Everywhere it hurts
I am going out
Because the heat kills me
My sweet heart if I deserve it
Give me a flower from your bush

El Pájaro Cú

Traditional *son* that is dedicated to the Pájaro Cú,
a bird from Veracruz.

Pájaro Cú placentero
De matizados colores
Anda y dile a mi lucero
Que reciba mis amores
Que por amarle me muero
Hay de todas las pasiones
Quiero la tuya
Por que con tus amores
Mi alma se arrulla
Eres mi prenda querida
Y yo tu pájaro cú
Arrímame la boquita
Y hagamos cu cu ru cu

Translation

Pleasant pájaro cu
Of nuanced colors
Go and tell my star
That receives my loves
Because I die to love her
Of all the passions
I prefer yours
Because if you love me
My soul gets cooing
You are what I love most
And I am your pajaro cu
Bring up your little mouth
And let's make cucurru cu

El Buscapies

A traditional *son* that is played after midnight during a *fandango*. The piece evokes superstition among those at the *fandango* because it's about a mysterious dancer who appears on the *tarima* and turns out to be the devil. Those at the *fandango* sing divine verses to drive the devil away.

Ave María, que ave, ave
De tan alta jerarquía
Ave María Dios te salve
Dios te salve ave Maria
Asi gritaban las viejas
Cuando el Diablo aparecia

Translation

Hail Mary, hail, hail
Of such high hierarchy
Hail Mary God save you
God save you hail Mary
So that old ladies shouted
When the devil appeared

Bemba y Tablao
By Patricio Hidalgo

This *son* is dedicated to the African influence of this music.
Bemba refers to the lips and *tarima* to the drum beats that dancers
produce with their heels.

Tarima Tumba y cajón
de donde viene tu encanto
me viene del corazón
del negro sereno y santo
Te vi cruzar la montaña
Te vi bajar el camino
A la zafra de la caña
Donde canta el campesino

Translation

Dance board, conga and drum box
Where does your charm comes from
It comes from the heart
From the serene and holy blacks

I saw you crossing the mountain
I saw you go down the path
To the cane harvest
Where the peasant sings

Son de Las Poblanas

A traditional *son* dedicated to the women from the state of Puebla, who are known for their weeping. In some cases, they are hired to weep at funerals.

Si yo me llego a morir
Tristes quedaran los llanos
Y les digo a mis hermanos
Que es todito mi sentir
Que me coman los gusanos

Lloren y lloren poblanas
Corazones de manzana
Que me van a dar la muerte
Mañana por la mañana
Y si me llego a morir
Lloren mujeres poblanas

Translation

If I got to die
The plains will be sad
And I tell my brothers
What is my whole feeling
That I want to be fed to the worms

Cry and cry poblanas
Women with apple hearts
Because they are going to kill me
Tomorrow in the morning
And if I end up dying
Cry poblanas for me

Conga Patria

By Patricio Hidalgo

This piece features the conga rhythm, an African rhythm that can be found in *son jarocho* music. It is dedicated to Mexico, as it undergoes a period of struggle and instability.

Quien dijo que habías perdido
Tu dignidad y tu historia
Quien dijo que tu memoria
Tan solo es polvo y olvido
Mira que el sol ha traído
Rayos de luz a tu huerta
Tu no eres patria muerta
Tienes corazón y vida
Y si te encuentras dormida
Despierta patria despierta

Translation

Who said that you had lost
Your dignity and your history
Who said that your memory
It's just dust and forgetting
Look that the sun has brought

Rays of light to your orchard
You are not dead fatherland
You have heart and life
And if you find yourself asleep
Wake up homeland wake up

Las Patronas
By Patricio Hidalgo

This song is about the women that feed the migrants that travel on the train, which is known as "The Beast," that runs from Southwest Mexico to the North. These women prepare plastic bags with food, and they toss them to the migrants when the train passes by. This is one of the most valuable acts of humanity these migrants encounter during their journey.

Deje mi casita
Mi tierra y mi arado
Hoy traigo en la bestia
Mi sueño dorado

Alla por la via
Vienen mas de cien,
Y vienen rezando
Arriba de un tren

Chorus
Hasta las Patronas
Muchos llegaran
Hasta las patronas
Muchos llegaran

Donde la esperanza
Se convierte en pan
Donde la esperanza
Se convierte en pan

Por el horizonte
Venimos cantando
Nuestro sueño roto
Se va desangrando

Emigra la luna
Y también el sol
Emigra la vida
Y también el amor

Translation

I left my little house
My land and my plow
Today I bring in the beast
My golden dream

Over the train track
More than one hundred are coming
They all come praying
On the roof of the train

Chorus
All the way to the Patronas
Many will come
All the way to the Patronas
Many will come

Where their hope
Will become bread
Where their hope
Will become bread

Through the horizon
We come singing
And our broken dream
Goes away bleeding

The moon migrates
So does the sun
Life migrates
So does love

Xalapa Bang!

Lyrics by Luis Villalobos

Oye! El país huele muy mal,
a poder que oprime la libertad,
hoy mi gente me recuerda una vez mas,
a Salvador Allende y al asesino Díaz Ordaz.

Pues han llegado con tanques, garrotes y aviones para "dialogar,"
y al que ponga resistencia lo desaparece el "halcón" judicial.

Y al mostrar bandera de paz,
nos han lanzado bombas de gas,
Aaaaaay! Vienen a aplastar a su gente, bang! bang! bang!

Anteayer, irrumpieron en mi hogar,
los soldados de plástico y de metal,

hoy llegaron frente a la universidad,
y pisotearon barricada y dignidad.

Van sometiendo países bajo un presidente que está corrompido,
se han de podrir en lombrices por lo que han robado a este México herido!

Somos pueblo, estamos unidos,
somos Juárez, no nos rendimos,
No! Y ésta es la canción de mi gente, bang! bang! bang!

Sale un canto Veracruzano,
pa'todo el pueblo Mexicano,
yo denuncio fraude y violencia
y si me matan por mi consciencia
sé…que el cobarde no hace la historia, bang! bang! bang!
Xalapa bang!

Translation

Wake up! Our country reeks again,
It's the reeking of the powerful oppressing freedom,
it reminds me of what happened to Salvador Allende,
and the students murdered by Díaz Ordaz.

You see, they've come armed with planes, tanks, and guns…ready to
*   "negotiate,"*
but the hawks swiftly silence anyone who dares to resist.

We marched waving our white flags,
but in response, they threw gas grenades at us,
Alas! They're here to crush their own people, bang! bang! bang!

Just yesterday, they broke into my home,
a hundred soldiers covered in plastic and metal,

Lyrics

today they breached the University,
stomping over wooden barricades and human dignity.

We see this pattern everywhere, subjugating countries under corrupt presidents,
I'm sure they'll rot amongst worms for everything they've done
to my wounded Mexico!

We are the nation, we are united,
We are all Juarez and will not surrender,
No! And this song is for all of my people, bang! bang! bang!

Let this message from Veracruz,
reach all across Mexico:
I denounce fraud and violence in my country,
and if I shall be murdered because of my ideals,
I die in peace, for history was never written with cowardice, bang! bang!
bang!
Xalapa bang!

Notes:

* Salvador Allende: Democratically elected president of Chile, assassinated in 1973 during a coup d'état with the aid of the United States. Later replaced by general and dictator Augusto Pinochet.

* Diaz Ordaz: 49th president of Mexico. Diaz Ordaz was responsible for the occupation of the National Autonomous University of Mexico and the arrest of several students, leading to the shooting of hundreds of unarmed protesters during the Tlatelolco massacre in downtown Mexico City on October 2, 1968.

* "Hawk": Undercover military personnel.

* Benito Juarez (referred to in the song simply as: Juarez): 26th president of Mexico, from rural indigenous origins. Widely regarded as one of Mexico's best presidents and a preeminent symbol of Mexican nationalism and resistance to foreign intervention.

El Pijul

Son tradicional Veracruzano
Arreglo original de Luis Villalobos

El norte y el sur cantando, tornan la atmósfera azul,
que cruzando la frontera (x2) ya nos íbamos quedando,
Ay, laralalalay!

Preso me llevan a mí, preso por ningún delito,
si todos somos iguales (x2) dime; ¿cómo te lo explico?
Ay, laralalalay!

Soy de tierra donde se ama y donde se ve la luz,
soy del cantón de Ozuluama, estado de Veracruz, república Mexicana,
Ay, laralalalay!

Translation

Traditional song from Veracruz
Original arrangement by Luis Villalobos

North and south singing together, tinting the atmosphere deep blue,
we sing of those who almost lost their lives, crossing the border and the desert,
Ay, laralalalay!

They are taking me captive, arrested for no crime,
if we are all truly equal, tell me…how does this make any sense?
Ay, laralalalay!

I am from a land of love, where light still shines,
I hail from the coastal town of Ozuluama, in Veracruz state, Mexico,
Ay, laralalalay!

Amor Sin Fronteras

Lyrics by Alberto Kreimerman
Courtesy Kibalion Publishing
Lyrics and translation by Alberto Kreimerman

En Busca de un sueño dejé mi pueblito
Yo era muy joven, quería triunfar
Todos me decían, allí del otro lado
La cosa es mas fácil lo puedes lograr.

Y me fui pal Norte, conocí otra gente
Y en esa nueva tierra forme yo mi hogar
Nacieron mis hijos, amé a dos banderas
Y segui luchando para progresar

Amor sin fronteras, sin miedos, sin odios
Somos gente buena, no nos quieras mal
Dios nos hizo iguales y nos dio derechos
Que nadie en la tierra nos puede quitar

Amor sin fronteras, progresemos juntos
Tu me necesitas igual que yo a ti
Yo a ti te respeto y exijo lo mismo
Amor sin fronteras, amor es la paz.
No oculto mi origen, mi piel ni mi raza
Limpie yo tus pisos, cuide tu jardín
cocine tu comida, pinte yo tu casa
Construí caminos y fui tu chofer.

Como muchos otros sembré yo tus tierras
Cuide de tus hijos, arreglé tu hogar
A mi me llamabas si tenías problemas
No me digas ahora....que soy ilegal

146

Amor sin fronteras, sin miedos, sin odios
Somos gente buena, no nos quieras mal
Dios nos hizo iguales y nos dio derechos
que nadie en la tierra nos puede quitar.

Amor sin fronteras, progresemos juntos
Tu me necesitas igual que yo a ti
Yo a ti te respeto y exijo lo mismo
Amor sin fronteras, amor es la paz.

Translation

Love without borders

I left my home town in search of a dream
I was so young and wanted to succeed
Everyone used to tell me that on the other side
Things were so much better and I had to try

So I traveled north and met the people
And in this new land I formed my home
I gave birth to my children and I love two flags
And I continued to struggle in hopes to progress.

I don't hide my heritage, yes I am Mexican
I cleaned your floors and painted your house
I cooked your food, take care of your garden
I built yours roads and I was your driver

Like many others, I planted your land
Took care of your children and I fixed your home
You always call me if you had any problems
Don't tell me now that I am illegal.

Love without borders, without fear, without hate
You know we're good people, don't treat me bad
God makes us brothers with rights that nobody could take away

Love without borders, let's progress together
You know that I need you just like you need me
I really respect you and demand you respect
Love without borders because love is peace

Hummingbird Blues

Lyrics by Kabir Sehgal

Gente de la frontera,
Serenata la barrera,
Aves de la frontera,
Vuelan alto sin barrera.

Chorus:
Song bird,
Give us your last word.
Red king,
Give us your last wing.
Sing right,
Into the bright light.
Fly high,
Into the night sky.

Translation

People of the border,
Serenade the barrier,
Birds of the border,
(They) fly high without barrier.

Line in the Sand

Trying to look past this thing that's between us,
Wondering when all the anger will fade,
The stars look the same from where we are standing,
Why can't we fix this mess we've made

Let's not forget that our fates are as one,
Just because
We feel numb and betrayed

There is love,
There must be,
Something good something strong
Between you and me
There is hope
We must try
If we don't we'll regret it
The rest of our lives

Side by side,
Forever,
You and me,
We are stronger
Together

Hoping to find a path to forgiveness,
Knowing that pride always gets in the way,
We all want a place where it's safe to be human,
The welcome embrace of a brand new day

Let's not allow what we have to be lost
Just because
Of what someone might say

There is love,
There must be,
Something good something strong
Between you and me
There is hope
We must try
If we don't we'll regret it
The rest of our lives

BIOGRAPHIES

Kabir Sehgal is a *New York Times* and *Wall Street Journal* bestselling author of twelve books, including five non-fiction works such as *Coined* and *Jazzocracy*; six children's books with his mother such as *A Bucket of Blessings* and *The Wheels on the Tuk*; and poetry book *Home* written with Deepak Chopra. He is a contributor to *CNBC*, *Fortune*, and *Harvard Business Review*. He has also written for *The New York Times*, *Foreign Policy*, and *Newsweek*. He has appeared on CNN, PBS, NPR, CNBC, Bloomberg, among other media outlets.

A multi-Grammy and Latin Grammy Award winning producer, he has collaborated with Chucho Valdés, Wynton Marsalis, Ted Nash, Joey Alexander, among others. He is also a composer and musician who wrote an opera on the European debt crisis.

Previously, he worked as a vice president at J.P. Morgan in emerging market equities, where he helped place the Alibaba IPO. Sehgal is a US Navy veteran and reserve officer who served on active duty with special operations in the Middle East. He is a graduate of Dartmouth College and the London School of Economics. He lives in New York City.

 **Arturo O'Farrill** is a pianist, composer, educator, and founder and artistic director of the nonprofit Afro Latin Jazz Alliance. He leads its resident ensemble, the Afro Latin Jazz Orchestra. O'Farrill has won four Grammy Awards and two Latin Grammy Awards—including winning the "Best Instrumental Composition" category twice.

O'Farrill received his formal musical education at the Manhattan School of Music, Brooklyn College Conservatory, and the Aaron Copland School of Music at Queens College.

He began his career as the pianist with the Carla Bley Big Band from 1979 through 1983. He later performed with Dizzy Gillespie, Wynton Marsalis, and Harry Belafonte.

O'Farrill performs throughout the world as a solo artist and also with his orchestra, as well as smaller ensembles. As an educator, he has taught seminars and workshops throughout the world for students and teachers of all levels. He has performed at the Kennedy Center for the Performing Arts, Boston Symphony Hall, the Newport Jazz Festival, the Joyce Theater (with Ballet Hispanico), Megaron Concert Hall (Athens, Greece), and at New York's Symphony Space, where he and his Afro Latin Jazz Orchestra have been in residence since 2007. He has received commissions from Jazz at Lincoln Center, The Philadelphia Music Project, the New York State Council on the Arts, and the Apollo Theater.

CREDITS

Photos

Cover: © 2018 by Kabir Sehgal

Book jacket: Jorge Francisco Castillo

Arturo O'Farrill photo: Laura Marie

Book interior photos: Varda Bar-Kar, Jorge Francisco Castillo, Saad Khan, Pedro González Kühn, Matthew Porwoll, Gustavo Vargas Ramírez, Kabir Sehgal, and Kashi Sehgal

Music

Full music credits can be found in the physical two-CD package and online.

Audiobook

Primary Artists & Readers: Kabir Sehgal, Douglas Brinkley

Produced by Cheryl Smith and Kabir Sehgal

Directed by Matt Longoria

Recorded by Sal Barone and Rafa Sardina

Post Production by Beatstreet NYC

Akua Dixon, Alberto Villalobos, Regina Carter, Ernesto Villalobos rehearsing in Tijuana

Ernesto Villalobos, Alberto Villalobos, Claudia Montes, and Jorge Francisco Castillo play music while walking through New York

ACKNOWLEDGMENTS

First and foremost, eternal thanks to Jorge Francisco Castillo for his vision in creating the Fandango Fronterizo festival. He is the inspiration for this whole project, and he has been a magnificent partner at every step. Whenever a new challenge would arise, he rose to the occasion with grace and strength. He didn't quite know what he was signing up for when I reached out to him and asked to partner on a project. Thanks for your faith and trust, *hermano* Jorge.

Arturo and I also want to thank all the organizers of the Fandango Fronterizo festival. Some of these kind and generous people include Edna Martinez, Jacob Hernandez, Citali Canales, Adrian Florido, Roxana Guajardo, Carolina Martinez, Marcos Lopez, Gabriela Muñoz. Also want to thank Angel Perea, Raul Candelario, Jorge Chausse, Guatavo Vargas, Josafat Reyes, Christian Mariche.

A special and sincerest thanks to the *son jarocho* musicians who opened up their homes and hearts to us. Arturo and I fell in love with *son jarocho* music, and we have all of you to thank: Patricio Hidalgo, Ramón Gutiérrez, Tacho Utrera, Fernando Guadarrama, Wendy Cao Romero (Maria Claudia Cao Romero Alcalá), Martha Vega Hernandez, Alfredo Herrera (Godo), Padi Jackson, Eduardo Castellanos, Minerva Alejandra Velez, Gabriel Garcia, Zenen Zeferino, Claudia Montes, Julia del Palacio, Paula Sanchez, Bruce Markow. A special thanks to Claudia for helping with translations.

Dearest Arturo O'Farrill, whose vision and virtuosity are second to none. It's an incredible honor to work and learn from you. Thank you for being a trailblazer and taking on projects of meaning and infusing your art with heart. I also want to thank all the members of the Afro Latin Jazz Orchestra: Vincent Cherico, Jim Seeley, Seneca Black, Bryan Davis, David Neves, Amer "Rocky" Abudlrahman, Frank Cohen, Earl McIntyre, Rafi Malkiel, Ivan Renta, Chad Lefkowitz-Brown,

Larry Bustamante, Carly Maldonado, Keisel Jimenez Leyva, Alexa Tarantino, Gregg August, Alejandro Aviles, Scott Englebright. Also: Josep Sanchez Pons, Sharon Moe-Miranda, David Oquendo, Lívio Almeida.

What made this project truly unique was collaborating with venerable guest artists who enriched the music with their imagination and creativity. Thank you to Regina Carter, Antonio Sanchez, Akua Dixon, Ernesto Villalobos, Alberto Villalobos, Luis Villalobos, Rahim AlHaj, Sahba Motallebi, Mandy Gonzalez, Ana Tijoux, Issa Malluff, Sourena Sefati, Humberto Manuel Flores Gutierrez, Jose Gurria-Cardenas, "Cenzoltle" (Tijuana Youth Chorus); and Young People's Chorus of New York City.

Thank you to the Afro Latin Jazz Alliance, an arts organization that provides educational opportunities and artistic programming to advance music of the rich Afro-Latin tradition. Thank you to the board, leadership, and staff: Marietta Ulacia, Felipe Tristan, Austin Kruczek, Jelani Buckner, Andrea Thompson, Dana Malseptic, Richard Miller, Amy Morales-Lara. A special thanks to Eric Taller for his steadfast patience as our production manager who handled the nuts and bolts of the operations.

Thank you to the entire production and engineering team and our friends: Saad Khan, Nicolas Rodriguez-Brizuela, Alison Deane, Zach O'Farrill, Adam O'Farrill, Rafa Sardina, Rafa's engineering team, Travis Brown, Teresa Barger, Aditya Srinath, Jesper Koll, Andrew Whitehouse, Dorie Clark, Alisa Cohn, David Levanson, Caitlin Levanson, Jared O'Connell, Doug Davis, Jason Flom, Asanka Pathiraja, Jim Allen, Rotimi Alakija, Shayne Ebudo, Alex Perfall, Ashley Perfall, Felix Perfall, Lynne Fowler, Maulik Zaveri, Imran Maskatia, Vikram Grover, Anamika Mandal, Jay Mandal, Fahad Khan, Maria Negrete, Craig Hyman, Jose Garcia, Ben Michaelis,

Jana Herzen, Dan Chamby, Etsuko Chamby, Jerry Bias, Sarah Armstrong, David Bonfili, George Iwanicki, Stephen Dembitzer, Fred Miller, Myles Weinstein, Sumaq Alvarado-del Aguila, Tom Frouge. The Gilman Foundation, John Arnhold and the Arnhold Foundation, The Aaron Copland Fund for Music, the New York Public Library, and Birdland.

Thank you to Varda Bar-Kar, Pedro González Kühn, Matthew Porwoll, Raquel Gallego, Melissa Uscanga, Rodrigo Álvarez Flores, Liye Leonor Rivera Melo, Sergio Valdes, Claudio Bautista, Diego Sandez, Johnny Hernandez, Andrés Acosta, Viktor Weiszhaupt, Jack Torella, Josh Ralph, Alberto Kreimerman, and Geoffrey Menin.

Eternal gratitude for Gretchen Young and Anthony Goff for believing in this project since inception, as well as their colleagues at Hachette Audio and Grand Central Publishing. Thank you to Michael Pietsch, Katherine Stopa, Emily Rosman, Cindy Joy, Cheryl Smith. Thank you to Steven Ruchefsky who dreams big and his team at Resilience Music Alliance (RMA) including Jeff Moskow and Jay Gilbert. RMA has been an important partner throughout.

We would also like to thank Sabrina Arredondo Grosvenor, Volaris, Boris Gartner, Nicolas Mamboury, Garron Hansen, Maximo Juda, Genoma Labb, Maher Al-haffar, Alejandro Scannapieco, Daniela Lecuona-Torras, Ben Walton, and Lucy Ana Walton.

Thank you to the Casa de la Cultura in Playas de Tijuana which generously provided space for us to rehearse and record in Tijuana. And to Stephen Webber and Power Station studios in New York City.

Thank you to mentors Douglas Brinkley and Andrew Young. Doron Weber, R. P. Eddy, Manu Chawla, Devika Chawla, Gil Goldstein, Alexandra Parker, Dennis D'Amico, Alan Thompson, Michael Owen, Bill vanden Heuvel, Douglas Dicconson, Jackie Niedbala, Bella Maytorena, Shannon O'Neil, Sofia Ramirez, Serge Morrell, Greer

Baxter, Lou D'Ambrosio, Sandy Jacobs, Alex Ohtli, Greg Behrman, Elyssa Dole, Kate Dinota, Melissa Herman, Faiza Chowdhury. Thank you to dearest Ariana Pieper, who is both supportive and brilliant, and a master performer on the *quijada de burro*. Thank you to all the musicians, production staff, friends, and families who supported this project.

And to my loving family who have supported me throughout: Surishtha Sehgal, R. K. Sehgal, Kashi Sehgal (who learned the *zapateado* dance at the Fandango Fronterizo festival).

Last but not least, the dancing horse that clicked to the music outside the Casa de la Cultura.

Diwaar (Wall)

by Saad Khan

Color and convergence
Letters and music
Challenge and response
Classic and Fusion

Come and Fandango
Angels and Earth
Borders and walls
Origins and birth

Syncopated rhythm
Cantar como un[*]
Huma zud byayen[†]
Kun-fa ya kun[‡]

---

[*]   Spanish: To sing as one
[†]   Farsi: everyone come quick
[‡]   Arabic: Be and it is

BIBLIOGRAPHY

Abrams, Jason. "Timeline." Greater Big Bend Coalition. November 17, 2017. https://greaterbigbend.wordpress.com/international-park-timeline-2/.

"The Adams-Onis Treaty of 1819." Sons of Dewittt Colony Texas. Accessed May 31, 2018. http://www.sonsofdewittcolony.org//adamonis.htm.

Aguila, Emma, Alisher Akhmedjonov, Ricardo Basurto-Davila, Krishna B. Kumar, Howard J. Shatz, and Sarah Kups. *United States and Mexico: Ties That Bind, Issues That Divide*. Santa Monica: RAND Corporation, 2012.

Allen, L. S. *Collaboration in the Borderlands: The Malpai Borderlands Group*. *Rangelands* 28, no. 3 (2006): 17–21.

Amadeo, Kimberly. "Why NAFTA's Six Advantages Outweigh Its Six Disadvantages." *The Balance*. March 06, 2018. https://www.thebalance.com/nafta-pros-and-cons-3970481.

Ambar, Saladin. "Woodrow Wilson: Foreign Affairs | Miller Center." Miller Center. Accessed May 31, 2018. https://millercenter.org/president/wilson/foreign-affairs.

AMLO. "Speech by AMLO in Los Angeles, California." Speech, Plaza Olvera, Los Angeles, February 12, 2017. https://lopezobrador.org.mx/2017/02/12/speech-by-amlo-in-los-angeles-california/.

"Analysis | In 466 Days, President Trump Has Made over 3,000 False or Misleading Claims." *The Washington Post*. Accessed May 31, 2018. https://www.washingtonpost.com/graphics/politics/trump-claims-database/?utm_term=.b3f44875a6ff

Anderson, Jon Lee. "How Mexico Deals with Trump." *The New Yorker*. May 31, 2018. https://www.newyorker.com/magazine/2017/10/09/mexico-in-the-age-of-trump.

"Articles of the Decree of April 1830." *The Portal to Texas History*. Accessed May 31, 2018. https://education.texashistory.unt.edu/lessons/notebook/LawApril/docs/LawApril_Articles.pdf.

Barclay, Eliza, and Sarah Frostenson. "The Ecological Disaster That Is Trump's Border Wall: A Visual Guide." *Vox*. October 29, 2017. https://www.vox.com/energy-and-environment/2017/4/10/14471304/trump-border-wall-animals.

Barclay, Eliza. "Congress Is Quietly Letting Trump Bulldoze a Butterfly Refuge to Build a Border Wall." *Vox*. March 28, 2018. https://www.vox.com/2018/3/28/17152644/trump-border-wall-texas-environment-refuge-butterflies.

Barrett, Rick. "Dairy Farms Fear Trump's Immigration Policies." *Milwaukee Journal Sentinel*. March 07, 2017. https://www.jsonline.com/story/money/business/2017/03/06/dairy-farms-fear-trumps-immigration-policies/98700808/.

Bibliography

Bennet, James. "POLITICS: PATRICK J. BUCHANAN; Candidate's Speech Is Called Code for Controversy." *The New York Times*. February 25, 1996. Accessed May 31, 2018. https://www.nytimes.com/1996/02/25/us/politics-patrick-j-buchanan-candidate-s-speech-is-called-code-for-controversy.html.

Bier, David. "Why the Wall Won't Work." Cato Institute. April 10, 2017. https://www.cato.org/publications/commentary/why-wall-wont-work.

Blazeski, Garon. "Pancho Villa Is Reported to Have Died Saying, 'Don't Let It End like This. Tell Them I Said Something.'" *The Vintage News*. July 15, 2017. Accessed 2. https://www.thevintagenews.com/2017/07/16/pancho-villa-is-reported-to-have-died-saying-dont-let-it-end-like-this-tell-them-i-said-something/.

"Border Patrol History." US Customs and Border Protection. March 24, 2018. https://www.cbp.gov/border-security/along-us-borders/history.

"Border Wall Information." National Butterfly Center. https://www.nationalbutterflycenter.org/about-nbcmaps-directions/9-national-butterfly-center/258-border-wall-information.

Bose, Jonaki, Sarra L. Hedden, Rachel N. Lipari, and Eunice Park-Lee. "Key Substance Use and Mental Health Indicators in the United States: Results From the 2015 National Survey on Drug Use and Health." Substance Abuse and Mental Health Service Administration (SAMHSA). September 2016. https://www.samhsa.gov/data/sites/default/files/NSDUH-FFR1-2015/NSDUH-FFR1-2015/NSDUH-FFR1-2015.pdf.

Bosque, Melissa Del. "National Butterfly Center Sues Trump Administration Over Border Wall." *The Texas Observer*. December 12, 2017. https://www.texasobserver.org/national-butterfly-center-sues-trump-administration-border-wall/.

Brown, Patricia L. "Sharing Music Across the US-Mexico Border's Metal Fence." *The New York Times*. December 21, 2017. Accessed May 31, 2018. https://www.nytimes.com/2016/05/30/arts/music/sharing-music-across-the-us-mexico-borders-metal-fence.html.

Buchalski, Michael R., Asako Y. Navarro, Walter M. Boyce, T. Winston Vickers, Mathias W. Tobler, Lisa A. Nordstrom, Jorge Alaníz García, Daphne A. Gille, Maria Cecilia T. Penedo, Oliver A. Ryder, and Holly B. Ernest. "Genetic Population Structure of Peninsular Bighorn Sheep (Ovis Canadensis Nelsoni) Indicates Substantial Gene Flow across US–Mexico Border." *Biological Conservation* 184 (April 2015): 218–28. doi:10.1016/j.biocon.2015.01.006.

Burnett, John. "Mexico Worries That A New Border Wall Will Worsen Flooding." *NPR*. April 25, 2017. Accessed May 31, 2018. https://www.npr.org/2017/04/25/525383494/trump-s-proposed-u-s-mexico-border-wall-may-violate-1970-treaty.

Bibliography

Burnett, John. "Arrests For Illegal Border Crossings Hit 46-Year Low." *NPR*. December 05, 2017. https://www.npr.org/2017/12/05/568546381/arrests-for-illegal-border -crossings-hit-46-year-low.

Carrigan, William. "The History of Anti-Mexican Violence And Lynching." *NPR* (podcast), March 17, 2017. https://www.npr.org/2017/03/17/520576256/the -history-of-anti-mexican-violence-and-lynching.

Carrigan, William D., and Clive Webb. "The Lynching of Persons of Mexican Origin or Descent in the United States, 1848–1928." *Journal of Social History,* 37, no. 2 (2003): 411–38.

Carrigan, William D., and Clive Webb. *Forgotten Dead: Mob Violence against Mexicans in the United States, 1848–1928.* New York: Oxford University Press, 2013.

Carswell, Cally. "Trump's Wall May Threaten Thousands of Plant and Animal Species on the US–Mexico Border." *Scientific American.* May 10, 2017. https://www. scientificamerican.com/article/trump-rsquo-s-wall-may-threaten-thousands-of -plant-and-animal-species-on-the-u-s-mexico-border/.

Casey, Edward S., and Mary Watkins. *Up Against The Wall: Re-Imagining the US-Mexico Border.* Austin: University of Texas Press, 2014.

Chishti, Muzaffar, Sarah Pierce, and Jessica Bolter. "The Obama Record on Deportations: Deporter in Chief or Not?" Migrationpolicy.org. March 22, 2017. Accessed May 31, 2018. https://www.migrationpolicy.org/article/obama-record -deportations-deporter-chief-or-not.

Chwe, Hanyu. "How Americans, Mexicans See Each Other Differs for Those Closer to Border." Pew Research Center. October 25, 2017. Accessed May 31, 2018. http:// www.pewresearch.org/fact-tank/2017/10/25/how-americans-mexicans-see -each-other-differs-for-those-closer-to-border/.

Clemens, Michael. "The US-Mexico Wage Gap Has Grown, Not Shrunk, under NAFTA. Awkward." Center For Global Development. March 17, 2015. https://www.cgdev. org/blog/us-mexico-wage-gap-has-grown-not-shrunk-under-nafta-awkward.

Clinton, William J. "William J. Clinton: Remarks at the Signing Ceremony for the Supplemental Agreements to the North American Free Trade Agreement— September 14, 1993." The American Presidency Project. September 14, 1993. http://www.presidency.ucsb.edu/ws/?pid=47070.

*Criminal Alien Statistics Information on Incarcerations, Arrests, and Costs.*Report no. GAO-11-187. United States Government Accountability Office. March 2011. https://www.gao.gov/assets/320/316959.pdf.

Danelo, David J. *The Border: Exploring the US-Mexican Divide.* Mechanicsburg, PA: Stackpole Books, 2008.

Bibliography

Davidson, Paul. "Automation Could Kill 73 Million US Jobs by 2030." *USA Today*. November 29, 2017. https://www.usatoday.com/story/money/2017/11/29/automation-could-kill-73-million-u-s-jobs-2030/899878001/.

De Gortari, Carlos Salinas. "Salinas Speaks Out On Free Trade In an Exclusive Interview, Mexico's President Rebuffs Naysayers on NAFTA and Argues That the Agreement Will Produce Winners on Both Sides of the Rio Grande. He Knows His Economics." December 28, 1992. *Fortune Magazine*, http://archive.fortune.com/magazines/fortune/fortune_archive/1992/12/28/77310/index.htm.

Díaz-Sánchez, Micaela, and Alexandro D. Hernández. "The Son Jarocho as Afro-Mexican Resistance Music." *The Journal of Pan African Studies* 6, no. 1 (July 2013): 187–209. Accessed May 31, 2018. http://www.jpanafrican.org/docs/vol6no1/6.1-12SonJarocho.pdf.

Dungan, Ron. "A Moving Border, and the History of a Difficult Boundary." *USA Today*. Accessed May 31, 2018. https://www.usatoday.com/border-wall/story/us-mexico-border-history/510833001/.

Enchautegui, Maria E. "Immigrant and Native Workers Compete for Different Low-skilled Jobs." Urban Institute. March 25, 2016. https://www.urban.org/urban-wire/immigrant-and-native-workers-compete-different-low-skilled-jobs.

"Environmental Laws Waived for Border Fence." NBCNews.com. October 23, 2007. http://www.nbcnews.com/id/21432742/ns/us_news-environment/t/environmental-laws-waived-border-fence/#.WujnEojwY2w.

Epstein, Reid J. "Ga. Immigrant Crackdown Backfires." June 22, 2011. https://www.politico.com/story/2011/06/ga-immigrant-crackdown-backfires-057551.

Eriksson, Lindsey, and Melinda Taylor. "The Environmental Impacts of the Border Wall Between Texas and Mexico." 2008. https://law.utexas.edu/humanrights/borderwall/analysis/briefing-The-Environmental-Impacts-of-the-Border-Wall.pdf.

"Fact Sheet: The Secure Fence Act of 2006." The White House. October 26, 2016. https://georgewbush-whitehouse.archives.gov/news/releases/2006/10/20061026-1.html.

Felbab-Brown, Vanda. "The Wall: The Real Costs of a Barrier between the United States and Mexico." Brookings. September 15, 2017. https://www.brookings.edu/essay/the-wall-the-real-costs-of-a-barrier-between-the-united-states-and-mexico/#price-tag.

Fischer, Alan. "Border Fence Blocks Wildlife Movement, UA Study Finds." UANews. June 30, 2010. https://uanews.arizona.edu/story/border-fence-blocks-wildlife-movement-ua-study-finds.

Bibliography

Fisher, Max, and Amanda Taub. "Mexico's Record Violence Is a Crisis 20 Years in the Making." *The New York Times*. October 28, 2017. https://www.nytimes.com/2017/10/28/world/americas/mexico-violence.html.

Flagg, Anna. "The Myth of the Criminal Immigrant." *The New York Times*. March 30, 2018. https://www.nytimes.com/interactive/2018/03/30/upshot/crime-immigration-myth.html.

Flesch, Aaron D., Clinton W. Epps, James W. Cain III, Matt Clark, Paul R. Krausman, and John R. Morgart. "Potential Effects of the United States-Mexico Border Fence on Wildlife." *Conservation Biology* 24, no. 1 (January 15, 2010): 171–81. doi:10.1111/j.1523-1739.2009.01277.x.

Flores, Antonio. "How the US Hispanic Population Is Changing." Pew Research Center. September 18, 2017. http://www.pewresearch.org/fact-tank/2017/09/18/how-the-u-s- hispanic-population-is-changing/.

Flores-Silva, Dolores. "Son Jarocho, Rock and Roll, and Bridges between Cultures: A Conversation with Agustin Del Moral Tejeda." *World Literature Today*, 2015, 53–56.

"Franklin D. Roosevelt: Address at Monterrey, Mexico.—April 20, 1943." The American Presidency Project. Accessed May 31, 2018. http://www.presidency.ucsb.edu/ws/index.php?pid=16387.

Frey, William H. "The US Will Become 'Minority White' in 2045, Census Projects." Brookings. March 14, 2018. https://www.brookings.edu/blog/the-avenue/2018/03/14/the-us-will-become-minority-white-in-2045-census-projects/.

Gable, Eryn. "75 Years On, Effort to Create US-Mexico Park Hampered by Security Concerns." *The New York Times*. June 24, 2010. Accessed May 31, 2018. https://archive.nytimes.com/www.nytimes.com/gwire/2010/06/24/24greenwire-75-years-on-effort-to-create-us-mexico-park-ha-13949.html.

"Gadsden Purchase, 1853–1854." US Department of State. Accessed May 31, 2018. https://history.state.gov/milestones/1830-1860/gadsden-purchase.

GAO. "Firearms Trafficking: US Efforts to Combat Firearms Trafficking to Mexico Have Improved, but Some Collaboration Challenges Remain." US Government Accountability Office (US GAO). January 11, 2016. https://www.gao.gov/products/GAO-16-223.

Garip, Filiz. "Discovering Diverse Mechanisms of Migration: The Mexico-US Stream 1970–2000." *Population and Development Review* 38, no. 3 (2012): 393–433.

Gaskill, Melissa. "United States Border Fence Threatens Wildlife." Nature News. August 02, 2011. https://www.nature.com/news/2011/110802/full/news.2011.452.html.

Bibliography

Gomez, Luis. "Meet the Mexican Presidential Hopeful Who Campaigned in California." Sandiegouniontribune.com. March 9, 2018. http://www.sandiegouniontribune. com/opinion/the-conversation/sd-mexican-presidential-candidate-ricardo -anaya-campaign-california-20180309-htmlstory.html.

Gonzalez-Barrera, Ana, and Jens Manuel Krogstad. "What We Know about Illegal Immigration from Mexico." Pew Research Center. March 02, 2017. http:// www.pewresearch.org/fact-tank/2017/03/02/what-we-know-about-illegal -immigration-from-mexico/.

Greenwald, Noah, Brian Segee, Tierra Curry, and Curt Bradley. "A Wall in the Wild: The Disastrous Impact of Trump's Border Wall on Wildlife." May 2017. http://www.biologicaldiversity.org/programs/international/borderlands_and _boundary_waters/pdfs/A_ʿall_in_the_Wild.pdf.

Grillo, Ioan. "Mexican Drug Smugglers to Trump: Thanks!" *The New York Times*. May 5, 2017. https://www.nytimes.com/2017/05/05/opinion/sunday/mexican-drug -smugglers-to-trump-thanks.html?_r=0.

Grimberg, Salomon. "Frida Kahlo's Still Lifes: 'I Paint Flowers So They Will Not Die.'" *Woman's Art Journal* 25, no. 2 (Autumn 2004–Winter 2005): 25-30. doi: 10.2307/3566514.

Gunaratna, Shanika. "Trump's Border Wall Would Be 'Catastrophe' for Wildlife, Expert Says." CBS News. March 29, 2017. https://www.cbsnews.com/news/trump -mexican-border-wall-environmental-wildlife-catastrophe/.

Henderson, Peter V. N. "Woodrow Wilson, Victoriano Huerta, and the Recognition Issue in Mexico." *The Americas* 41, no. 2 (1984): 151–76.

"Here's What We Know About Trump's Mexico Wall." *Bloomberg*. February 13, 2013. https://www.bloomberg.com/graphics/2017-trump-mexico-wall/how-long -would-the-wall-be/.

"Hispanics in the US Fast Facts." CNN. March 22, 2018. https://www.cnn.com/2013 /09/20/us/hispanics-in-the-u-s-/index.html.

Homeland Security. "US-Mexico Bi-National Criminal Proceeds Study." ICE. Accessed May 31, 2018. https://www.ice.gov/doclib/cornerstone/pdf/cps-study.pdf.

"How Do Cartels Get Drugs into the US?" BBC News. December 03, 2015. http:// www.bbc.com/news/world-us-canada-34934574.

HSBC Global Research. "What if NAFTA breaks up?" November 16, 2017

Hufbauer, Gary, Cathleen Cimino, and Tyler Moran. "NAFTA at 20: Misleading Charges and Positive Achievements." PIIE. September 28, 2016. https://piie. com/publications/policy-briefs/nafta-20-misleading-charges-and-positive -achievements.

Bibliography

Hurst, Blake. "A Farmer's View of NAFTA." *National Review*. October 26, 2017. https://www.nationalreview.com/2017/10/nafta-farmers-case-trade-deal/.

Ingold, David, Chloe Whiteaker, Mira Rojanasakul, Hannah Recht, and Dean Halford. "Here's What We Know About Trump's Mexico Wall." Bloomberg. February 13, 2017. https://www.bloomberg.com/graphics/2017-trump-mexico-wall/how-many -people-currently-cross/.

Inserra, David. "The Wall Is Not Enough. Here's How to Solve Illegal Immigration." The Heritage Foundation. January 9, 2018. https://www.heritage.org/immigration/ commentary/the-wall-not-enough-heres-how-solve-illegal-immigration.

Jenkins, Nash. "Trump Got $1.6 Billion For Border Security. He Says It Isn't Enough." *Time*. March 22, 2018. http://time.com/5210780/congress-omnibus-border -security-wall-donald-trump/.

Johnson, Kristina, and Samuel Fromartz. "NAFTA's 'Broken Promises': These Farmers Say They Got The Raw End Of Trade Deal." NPR. August 07, 2017. https://www. npr.org/sections/thesalt/2017/08/07/541671747/nafta-s-broken-promises-these -farmers-say-they-got-the-raw-end-of-trade-deal.

"José Antonio Meade Secunda a Peña Nieto Y Le Pide Respeto a Donald Trump." Expansión. April 6, 2018. https://expansion.mx/video-politica/2018/04/06/jose -antonio-meade-secunda-a-pena-nieto-y-le-pide-respeto-a-donald-trump.

Kaylaw. "Gloria Anzaldúa's Borderlands/La Frontera: The Literary Barbwire Fence." *Transnational Theory and Criticism* (blog), September 29, 2014. http://blog.umd. edu/transnational14/2014/09/29/gloria-anzalduas-borderlandsla-frontera-the -literary-barbwire-fence/.

Kiely, Eugene. "Fact Check: Will President Trump's Border Wall Stop Drug Smuggling?" *USA Today*. August 31, 2017. https://www.usatoday.com/story/news/ politics/2017/08/31/fact-check-president-trump-border-wall-drug-smuggling /619865001/.

Kingston, John. "The Economic Impact of NAFTA—Frequently Asked Questions." S&P Global Market Intelligence. January 10, 2018. https://www.spglobal.com /our-insights/FAQ-The-Economic-Impact-of-NAFTA.html.

Kopan, Tal, Rene Marsh, and Gregory Wallace. "Trump Admin Waives Laws for Border Wall." CNN. August 02, 2017. https://www.cnn.com/2017/08/01/politics/ trump-waives-environmental-laws-border-wall/index.html.

Kopan, Tal. "Report: Trump Admin Taking Steps on Seizing Border Land." CNN. November 14, 2017. https://www.cnn.com/2017/11/13/politics/border-wall -eminent-domain /index.html.

Bibliography

Krauze, Enrique. "The April Invasion of Veracruz." *The New York Times*. April 20, 2014. https://www.nytimes.com/2014/04/21/opinion/krauze-the-april-invasion-of-veracruz.html.

Krogstad, Jens Manuel, Jeffrey S. Passel, and D'Vera Cohn. "5 Facts about Illegal Immigration in the US." Pew Research Center. April 27, 2017. http://www.pewresearch.org/fact-tank/2017/04/27/5-facts-about-illegal-immigration-in-the-u-s/.

Krugman, Paul. "The Uncomfortable Truth about NAFTA: Its Foreign Policy, Stupid." *Foreign Affairs* 72, no. 5 (1993): 13–19.

Landgrave, Michelangelo, and Alex Nowrasteh. "Criminal Immigrants: Their Numbers, Demographics, and Countries of Origin." Cato Institute. March 15, 2017. https://www.cato.org/publications/immigration-reform-bulletin/criminal-immigrants-their-numbers-demographics-countries.

Lasky, Jesse R., Walter Jetz, and Timothy H. Keitt. "Conservation Biogeography of the US-Mexico Border: A Transcontinental Risk Assessment of Barriers to Animal Dispersal." *Diversity and Distributions* 17, no. 4 (2011): 673–87. doi:10.1111/j.1472-4642.2011.00765.x.

Lee, Michelle Ye Hee. "Analysis | Donald Trump's False Comments Connecting Mexican Immigrants and Crime." *The Washington Post*. July 8, 2015. Accessed May 31, 2018. https://www.washingtonpost.com/news/fact-checker/wp/2015/07/08/donald-trumps-false-comments-connecting-mexican-immigrants-and-crime/?noredirect=on&utm_term=.6c671c95bcf0.

LoBello, Rick. "Coalition Renews Big Bend International Park Campaign." Rio Grande Chapter. October 25, 2016. http://www.riograndesierraclub.org/coalition-renews-big-bend-international-park-campaign/.

Loomis, Brandon. "A Border Wall Could Drive the Jaguar Extinct in America." Azcentral. May 23, 2018. https://www.azcentral.com/story/news/local/arizona-environment/2017/11/21/border-wall-could-drive-jaguar-extinct-america/480883001/.

Lopez, German. "In One Year, Drug Overdoses Killed More Americans than the Entire Vietnam War Did." *Vox*. June 6, 2017. https://www.vox.com/policy-and-politics/2017/6/6/15743986/opioid-epidemic-overdose-deaths-2016.

López, Gustavo. "Hispanics of Mexican Origin in the United States, 2013." Pew Research Center's Hispanic Trends Project. September 15, 2015. http://www.pewhispanic.org/2015/09/15/hispanics-of-mexican-origin-in-the-united-states-2013/.

Lopez, Mark Hugo. "In 2014, Latinos will surpass whites as largest racial/ethnic group in California." Pew Research Center. January 24, 2014. http://www.pewresearch.org/fact-tank/2014/01/24/in-2014-latinos-will-surpass-whites-as-largest-racialethnic-group-in-california/.

Bibliography

Mallonee, Laura. "Wanna See How Divided the Country Is? Visit the US-Mexico Border." *Wired*. August 24, 2017. https://www.wired.com/story/wanna-see-how-divided-the-country-is-visit-the-us-mexico-border/.

Marshall, Serena. "Obama Has Deported More People Than Any Other President." *ABC News*. August 29, 2016. http://abcnews.go.com/Politics/obamas-deportation-policy-numbers/story?id=41715661.

McBride, James, and Mohammed A, Sergie. "NAFTA's Economic Impact." Council on Foreign Relations. https://www.cfr.org/backgrounder/naftas-economic-impact.

"Mexicans Returning Home Outnumber Those Immigrating to US, Study Shows." *The Guardian*. November 19, 2015. https://www.theguardian.com/us-news/2015/nov/19/mexicans-returning-home-outnumber-those-immigrating-to-us-study-shows.

"Mexico Drug War Fast Facts." CNN. March 21, 2018. https://www.cnncom/2013/09/02/world/americas/mexico-drug-war-fast-facts/index.html.

"Mexico 'will Not Pay for US Border Wall'—President Enrique Pena Nieto." *BBC News*. January 26, 2017. http://www.bbc.com/news/av/world-latin-america-38753660/mexico-will-not-pay-for-us-border-wall-president-enrique-pena-nieto.

Mishima, Yukio. *Spring Snow*. New York: Alfred A. Knopf, 1972.

Montemayor, Gabriel Diaz. "Here's a Better Vision for the US-Mexico Border: Make the Rio Grande Grand Again." *The Conversation*. August 22, 2017. http://theconversation.com/heres-a-better-vision-for-the-us-mexico-border-make-the-rio-grande-grand-again-73111.

Náñez, Dianna M. "A Border Tribe, and the Wall That Will Divide It." *USA Today*. Accessed May 31, 2018. https://www.usatoday.com/border-wall/story/tohono-oodham-nation-arizona-tribe/582487001/.

Náñez, Dianna M. "Tohono O'odham Tribal Members Opposing Trump's Border Wall Take Fight to McCain." *Azcentral*. March 23, 2017. https://www.azcentral.com/story/news/politics/border-issues/2017/03/23/tohono-oodham-trump-border-wall/99550594/.

Navarro, Andrea. "Starbucks Sales at Mexico's Alsea Hit by Anti-Trump Sentiment." Bloomberg.com. April 27, 2017. https://www.bloomberg.com/news/articles/2017-04-27/starbucks-sales-at-mexico-s-alsea-hit-by-anti-trump-sentiment.

Nicol, Scott. "New Border Walls Designed to Flood Texas Towns." *The Texas Observer*. July 11, 2012. https://www.texasobserver.org/new-border-walls-designed-to-flood-texas-towns/.

167

Nieto, Alejandro Miranda. *Musical Mobilities: Son Jarocho and the Circulation of Tradition across Mexico and the United States.* Kindle ed. New York: Routledge, an Imprint of the Taylor & Francis Group, 2018.

Nixon, Ron. "By Land, Sea or Catapult: How Smugglers Get Drugs Across the Border." *The New York Times.* July 25, 2017. https://www.nytimes.com/2017/07/25/us/drugs-border-wall.html.

Nixon, Ron, and Fernanda Santos. "US Appetite for Mexico's Drugs Fuels Illegal Immigration." *The New York Times.* April 5, 2017. https://www.nytimes.com/2017/04/04/us/politics/us-appetite-for-mexicos-drugs-fuels-illegal-immigration.html.

"Notable Quotes of Sam Houston." Sam Houston Memorial Museum. Accessed May 31, 2018. http://samhoustonmemorialmuseum.com/history/quotes.html.

O'Neil, Shannon K. *Two Nations Indivisible: Mexico, the United States, and the Road Ahead.* New York: Oxford University Press, 2015.

Pancho, Jose. "Tohono O'odham-English Dictionary." http://www.acsu.buffalo.edu/~mathiotm/Mathiot/Volume I.pdf.

"Partners in Protection of the Chihuahuan Desert." National Parks Service. February 24, 2015. https://www.nps.gov/bibe/learn/nature/mexareas.htm.

Paxman, Andrew. *Jenkins of Mexico: How a Southern Farm Boy Became a Mexican Magnate.* New York: Oxford University Press, 2017.

Paxman, Andrew. "The Return of Gringophobia." *Slate* magazine. May 29, 2017. http://www.slate.com/articles/news_and_politics/foreigners/2017/05/what_the_history_of_mexican_anti_americanism_can_tell_us_about_the_trump.html.

Porter, Jeremy D., and Michael Pemberton. "Key Substance Use and Mental Health Indicators in the United States: Results from the 2015 National Survey on Drug Use and Health." SAMHSA. September 2016. https://www.samhsa.gov/data/sites/default/files/NSDUH-FFR1-2015/NSDUH-FFR1-2015/NSDUH-FFR1-2015.pdf.

Rael, Ronald. "Boundary Line Infrastructure." *Thresholds* 20 (2012): 75–82.

Ramirez, Chris, and John C. Moritz. "Border Homes, and the Wall That Would Tear Them Apart." *USA Today.* https://www.usatoday.com/border-wall/story/eminent-domain- trump-border-wall-rio-grande/638916001/.

"Ready to Take off Again?" *The Economist.* January 4, 2014. https://www.economist.com/news/briefing/21592631-two-decades-ago-north-american-free-trade-agreement-got-flying-start-then-it.

Rodríguez-Soto, Clarita, Octavio Monroy-Vilchis, Luigi Maiorano, Luigi Boitani, Juan Carlos Faller, Miguel Á. Briones, Rodrigo Núñez, Octavio Rosas-Rosas,

Bibliography

Gerardo Ceballos, and Alessandra Falcucci. "Predicting Potential Distribution of the Jaguar (Panthera Onca) in Mexico: Identification of Priority Areas for Conservation." *Diversity and Distributions* 17, no. 2 (2011): 350–61.

Root, Jay. "When Americans Were Illegal Immigrants in Mexico." *The New York Times.* December 13, 2012. https://www.nytimes.com/2012/12/14/us/when-americans -were-illegal-immigrants-in-mexico.html?mtrref=www.google.com&gwh =AA4AEC20A2FDC8200695F431EAE8F5EE&gwt=pay.

Sands, Geneva. "Judge, Once Berated by Trump, Rules in Favor of Border Wall Waivers." ABC News. February 28, 2018. http://abcnews.go.com/Politics/judge-berated - trump-rules-favor-border-wall-waivers/story?id=53427234.

San Miguel, Guadalupe, Jr. *Brown, Not White: School Integration and the Chicano Movement in Houston.* College Station: Texas A&M University Press, 2005.

Seitz-Wald, Alex. "Actually, Salsa Dethroned Ketchup 20 Years Ago." *The Atlantic.* October 17, 2013. https://www.theatlantic.com/national/archive/2013/10/actua lly-salsa- dethroned-ketchup-20-years-ago/309844/.

Siler, Wes. "These Are the 111 Endangered Species Threatened by Trump's Wall." *Outside Online.* May 23, 2017. https://www.outsideonline.com/2075761/trumps -wall-threatens-111-endangered-species.

Sirotnak, Joe. "Binational Cooperation in the Big Bend Region." The George Wright Forum. 2011. http://www.georgewright.org/283sirotnak.pdf.

Soboroff, Jacob. "House Bill Bans Border Wall Construction in Federal Wildlife Refuge." NBCNews.com. March 22, 2018. https://www.nbcnews.com/politics/national- security/house-bill-bans-border-wall-construction-santa-ana-wildlife-refuge-n859191.

"Sociocultural Dimensions of Immigrant Integration." In *The Integration of Immigrants into American Society,* edited by Mary C. Waters and Marisa Gerstein Pineau, 303–44. Washington, DC: National Academies Press, 2015. https://www. nap.edu/read/21746/chapter/9#325.

Solis, Gustavo. "Drug Smuggling, and the Endless Battle to Stop It." *USA Today.* Accessed May 31, 2018. https://www.usatoday.com/border-wall/story/drug -trafficking-smuggling-cartels-tunnels/559814001/.

"Southwest Borderlands." National Museum of American History. May 3, 2018. http:// americanhistory.si.edu/many-voices-exhibition/new-americans-continuing -debates-1965–2000/southwest-borderlands.

St. John, Rachael. *Bridging National Borders in North America.* A. R. Benjamin H. Johnson, ed. Durham and London: Duke University Press, 2010.

Stein, Mark. *American Panic: A History of Who Scares Us and Why.* New York: St. Martin's Press, 2014.

Bibliography

Stout, David. "Bush Signs Bill Ordering Fence on Mexican Border." *The New York Times.* October 26, 2006. https://www.nytimes.com/2006/10/26/washington/27fencecnd.html.

Sundstrom, Ronald R. "Sheltering Xenophobia." *Critical Philosophy of Race*1, no. 1 (2013): 68–85. doi:10.5325/critphilrace.1.1.0068.

Taylor, Adam. "Mexican Views of the United States Drop to Record Low, Poll Finds." *The Washington Post.* January 18, 2018. Accessed May 31, 2018. https://www.washingtonpost.com/news/worldviews/wp/2018/01/18/mexican-views-of-the-united-states-drop-to-record-low-poll-finds/?utm_term=.dee7e14cd683.

Thomsen, Jacqueline. "Mexican-American Judge Who Trump Attacked Rules in Favor of Border Wall." *The Hill.* February 28, 2018. http://thehill.com/regulation/court-battles/375875-mexican-american-judge-that-trump-attacked-rules-in-favor-of-trumps.

"Timeline: US-Mexico Relations." Council on Foreign Relations. Accessed May 31, 2018. https://www.cfr.org/timeline/us-mexico-relations.

Time Staff. "Donald Trump's Presidential Announcement Speech." *Time.* June 16, 2015. Accessed May 31, 2018. http://time.com/3923128/donald-trump-announcement-speech/.

Tinoco, Armando. "María Félix 100th Anniversary: One Hundred Quotes To Honor The Biggest Diva Of Mexican Cinema." *Latin Times.* April 08, 2014. Accessed May 31, 2018. https://www.latintimes.com/maria-felix-100th-anniversary-one-hundred-quotes-honor-biggest-diva-mexican-cinema-164309.

Turner, Frederick C. "Anti-Americanism in Mexico, 1910–1913." *The Hispanic American Historical Review* 47, no. 4 (November 1967): 502–18. doi:10.1163/2468-1733_shafr_sim090210054.

Turner, Frederick C. *The Dynamic of Mexican Nationalism.* University of North Carolina Press, 1968.

Tyson, Timothy B. "The Civil Rights Stories We Need to Remember." *The New York Times.* May 19, 2017. https://www.nytimes.com/2017/05/19/books/review/he-calls-me-by-lightning-s-jonathan-bass.html.

USDA. "Infographic: US Agricultural Exports to Mexico, 2016." CAFTA-DR: A Trade Partnership That Works | USDA Foreign Agricultural Service. May 5, 2017. https://www.fas.usda.gov/data/infographic-us-agricultural-exports-mexico-2016.

US Department of Homeland Security. "DHS Issues Waiver to Expedite Border Construction Projects in San Diego Area." News release, August 1, 2017. Homeland Security. https://www.dhs.gov/news/2017/08/01/dhs-issues-waiver-expedite-border-construction-projects-san-diego-area.

Bibliography

US Department of the Interior. Big Bend National Park. "Secretaries Jewell, Guerra Celebrate the Binational Big Bend/Río Bravo Conservation Partnership, Two-Year Anniversary of Boquillas Port of Entry." News release, October 4, 2015. https://www.doi.gov/news/pressreleases/secretaries-jewell-guerra-celebrate-the-binational-big-bend-rio-bravo-conservation-partnership-two-year-anniversary-of-boquillas-port-of-entry.

Villarreal, M. Angeles, and Ian F. Fergusson. "The North American Free Trade Agreement (NAFTA)." FAS. May 24, 2017. https://fas.org/sgp/crs/row/R42965.pdf.

Villegas, Paulina. "Missing Mexicans' Case Shines Light on Military's Role in Drug War." *The New York Times.* April 30, 2018. https://www.nytimes.com/2018/04/30/world/ americas/mexico-missing-military-drugs.html.

Wagner, Dennis. "Border Violence, and the Families in Its Wake." *USA Today.* Accessed May 31, 2018. https://www.usatoday.com/border-wall/story/brian-terry-us-border- patrol-agent/560448001/.

"The Wall—An In-depth Examination of Donald Trump's Border Wall." *USA Today.* Accessed May 31, 2018. https://www.usatoday.com/border-wall/.

Waters, Mary C., and Marisa Gerstein. Pineau. *The Integration of Immigrants into American Society.* Washington, D.C.: National Academies Press, 2015.

Waxman, Olivia B. "Donald Trump, Immigration, Borders and the History of Walls." *Time.* January 30, 2017. http://time.com/4652770/donald-trump-immigration-walls-history/.

Whelan, Robbie. "Why Your Flat-Screen TV Would Cost More If NAFTA Ends." *The Wall Street Journal.* November 27, 2017. https://www.wsj.com/articles/why-your-flat-screen-tv-would-cost-more-if-nafta-ends-1511344800.

Worley, Will. "Mexicans Celebrate Easter by Blowing up Effigy of Donald Trump." *The Independent.* April 17, 2017. https://www.independent.co.uk/news/world/americas/mexico-city-burns-efigy-donald-trump-judas-iscariot-celebrate-easter-a7687701.html.

Woosnam, Kyle, Rebekka Dudensing, Dan Hanselka, and Seonhee An. "An Initial Examination of the Economic Impact of Nature…" U.S Fish and Wildlife Service. September 1, 2011. https://www.fws.gov/uploadedfiles/naturereport-mcallencvb-2011_508.pdf.

WSDBHome. Accessed June 1, 2018. http://stat.wto.org/TariffProfiles/MX_e.htm.

W. W. "Blame Mexico!" *The Economist.* August 18, 2015. https://www.economist.com/blogs/democracyinamerica/2015/08/donald-trump-immigration-reform.

Yardley, Jonathan. "'A Wicked War: Polk, Clay, Lincoln, and the 1846 US Invasion of Mexico' by Amy S. Greenberg." *The Washington Post.* November 24, 2012.

Bibliography

Accessed May 31, 2018. https://www.washingtonpost.com/opinions/a-wicked-war-polk-clay-lincoln-andthe-1846-us-invasion-of-mexico-by-amy-s-greenberg/2012/11/23/db678388-2dc7-11e2-9ac2-1c61452669c3_story.html?noredirect=on&utm_term=.7970bb7ef690.

Yee, Vivian, Kenan Davis, and Jugal K. Patel. "Here's the Reality About Illegal Immigrants in the United States." *The New York Times*. March 6, 2017. https://www.nytimes.com/interactive/2017/03/06/us/politics/undocumented-illegal-immigrants.html.

Zong, Jie, and Jeanne Batalova. "Mexican Immigrants in the United States." Migrationpolicy.org. March 17, 2016. https://www.migrationpolicy.org/article/mexican-immigrants-united-states#Income and Poverty.

Recording the band at the Casa de la Cultura in 2018

NOTES

Introduction

1   David J. Danelo, *The Border: Exploring the US-Mexican Divide* (Mechanicsburg, PA: Stackpole Books, 2008), xii.

2   Armando Tinoco, "María Félix 100th Anniversary: One Hundred Quotes To Honor The Biggest Diva Of Mexican Cinema," *Latin Times*, April 8, 2014, accessed May 31, 2018, https://www.latintimes.com/maria-felix-100th-anniversary-one -hundred-quotes-honor-biggest-diva-mexican-cinema-164309.

3   "Franklin D. Roosevelt: Address at Monterrey, Mexico.—April 20, 1943," The American Presidency Project, accessed May 31, 2018, http://www.presidency. ucsb.edu/ws/index.php?pid=16387.

4   Adam Taylor, "Mexican Views of the United States Drop to Record Low, Poll Finds," *The Washington Post*, January 18, 2018, accessed May 31, 2018, https:// www.washingtonpost.com/news/worldviews/wp/2018/01/18/mexican-views-of -the-united-states-drop-to-record-low-poll-finds/?utm_term=.dee7e14cd683.

5   *Time* Staff, "Donald Trump's Presidential Announcement Speech," *Time*, June 16, 2015, accessed May 31, 2018, http://time.com/3923128/donald-trump -announcement-speech/.

6   Ibid.

7   James Bennet, "Politics: Patrick J. Buchanan; Candidate's Speech Is Called Code for Controversy," *The New York Times*, February 25, 1996, accessed May 31, 2018, https://www.nytimes.com/1996/02/25/us/politics-patrick-j-buchanan-candidate -s-speech.is-called-code-for-controversy.html.

8   Michelle Ye Hee Lee, "Analysis | Donald Trump's False Comments Connecting Mexican Immigrants and Crime," *The Washington Post*, July 8, 2015, accessed May 31, 2018, https://www.washingtonpost.com/news/fact-checker/wp/2015/07/08/ donald-trumps-false-comments-connecting-mexican-immigrants-and-crime /?noredirect=on&utm_term=.6c671c95bcf0.

9   "In 466 Days, President Trump Has Made over 3,000 False or Misleading Claims," *The Washington Post*, accessed May 31, 2018, https://www.washingtonpost.com/ graphics/politics/trump-claims-database/?utm_term=.b3f44875a6ff.

10 Olivia B. Waxman, "Donald Trump, Immigration, Borders and the History of Walls," *Time*, January 30, 2017, http://time.com/4652770/donald-trump -immigration-walls-history/.

Chapter One: Fandango for the Future

1   Yukio Mishima, *Spring Snow* (New York: Alfred A. Knopf, 1972), 222.

2   Dolores Flores-Silva, "Son Jarocho, Rock and Roll, and Bridges between Cultures: A Conversation with Agustin Del Moral Tejeda," *World Literature Today*, 2015, 53–56.

3   Patricia L. Brown, "Sharing Music Across the US-Mexico Border's Metal Fence," *The New York Times*, May 29, 2017, https://www.nytimes.com/2016/05/30/arts/ music/sharing-music-across-the-us-mexico-borders-metal-fence.html.

4   Micaela Díaz-Sánchez and Alexandro D. Hernández, "The Son Jarocho as Afro-Mexican Resistance Music" *The Journal of Pan African Studies* 6, no. 1 (July 2013), http://www.jpanafrican.org/docs/ vol6no1/6.1-12SonJarocho.pdf.

5   Ibid.

6   Alejandro Miranda Nieto, *Musical Mobilities: Son Jarocho and the Circulation of Tradition across Mexico and the United States*, Kindle ed. (New York: Routledge, an Imprint of the Taylor & Francis Group, 2018), 7.

7   Ibid., 475.

8   Ibid., 10.

9   Patricia L. Brown, "Sharing Music Across the US-Mexico Border's Metal Fence," *The New York Times*, May 29, 2017, https://www.nytimes.com/2016/05/30/arts/ music/sharing-music-across-the-us-mexico-borders-metal-fence.html.

10 Hanyu Chwe, "How Americans, Mexicans See Each Other Differs for Those Closer to Border," Pew Research Center, October 25, 2017, accessed May 31, 2018, http://www.pewresearch.org/fact-tank/2017/10/25/how-americans-mexicans-see-each-other-differs-for-those-closer-to-border/.

11 Edward S. Casey and Mary Watkins, *Up Against The Wall: Re-Imagining the US-Mexico Border* (Austin: University of Texas Press, 2014), 207-210.

12 Speech was delivered at the LinkedIn Conference for Women of Color on April 11, 2018

Chapter 2: Requiem for the Borderlands

1   Kaylaw, "Gloria Anzaldúa's Borderlands/La Frontera: The Literary Barbwire Fence," *Transnational Theory and Criticism* (blog), September 29, 2014, http:// blog.umd.edu/transnational14/2014/09/29/gloria-anzalduas-borderlandsla -frontera-the-literary-barbwire-fence/.

2   Alan Fischer, "Border Fence Blocks Wildlife Movement, UA Study Finds,"
    UANews, June 30, 2010, https://uanews.arizona.edu/story/border-fence-blocks
    -wildlife-movement-ua-study-finds.

3   Dianna M. Náñez, "Tohono O'odham Tribal Members Opposing Trump's Border
    Wall Take Fight to McCain," Azcentral, March 23, 2017, https://www.azcentral.
    com/story/news/politics/border-issues/2017/03/23/tohono-oodham-trump
    -border-wall/99550594/.

4   Eliza Barclay and Sarah Frostenson, "The Ecological Disaster That Is Trump's
    Border Wall: A Visual Guide," Vox, October 29, 2017, https://www.vox.com/
    energy-and-environment/2017/4/10/14471304/trump-border-wall-animals.

    Jesse R. Lasky, Walter Jetz, and Timothy H. Keitt, "Conservation Biogeography
    of the US-Mexico Border: A Transcontinental Risk Assessment of Barriers
    to Animal Dispersal," Diversity and Distributions 17, no. 4 (2011): 673-687,
    doi:10.1111/j.1472-4642.2011.00765.x.

5   Ibid., 673–87.

6   Melissa Gaskill, "United States Border Fence Threatens Wildlife," Nature News,
    August 2, 2011, https://www.nature.com/news/2011/110802/full/news.2011.452.
    html.

7   Michael R. Buchalski et al., "Genetic Population Structure of Peninsular Bighorn
    Sheep (Ovis Canadensis Nelsoni) Indicates Substantial Gene Flow across US–
    Mexico Border," Biological Conservation 184 (April 2015): 218–28, doi:10.1016/j.
    biocon.2015.01.006.

8   Melissa Gaskill, "United States Border Fence Threatens Wildlife," Nature News,
    August 2, 2011, https://www.nature.com/news/2011/110802/full/news.2011.452.
    html.

9   Ibid.

10 Clarita Rodríguez-Soto et al., "Predicting Potential Distribution of the Jaguar
    (Panthera Onca) in Mexico: Identification of Priority Areas for Conservation,"
    Diversity and Distributions 17, no. 2 (January 30, 2011): 350–61, doi:10.1111/
    j.1472-4642.2010.00740.x.

11 Brandon Loomis, "A Border Wall Could Drive the Jaguar Extinct in America,"
    Azcentral, May 23, 2018, https://www.azcentral.com/story/news/local/arizona
    -environment/2017/11/21/border-wall-could-drive-jaguar-extinct-america
    /480883001/.

12 Ibid.

13 Aaron D. Flesch et al., "Potential Effects of the United States-Mexico Border
    Fence on Wildlife," Conservation Biology 24, no. 1 (2010): 171–81.

Notes

14 Noah Greenwald et al., "A Wall in the Wild: The Disastrous Impact of Trump's Border Wall on Wildlife," May 2017, 1–17, http://www.biologicaldiversity.org/ programs/ international/borderlands_and_boundary_waters/ pdfs/ A_Wall_in _the_Wild.pdf.

15 Lindsey Eriksson and Melinda Taylor, "The Environmental Impacts of the Border Wall Between Texas and Mexico," 2008, 1–10, The University of Texas at Austin School of Law—The Bernard and Audre Rapoport Center for Human Rights and Justice, https://law.utexas.edu/humanrights/borderwall/analysis/briefing -The-Environmental-Impacts-of-the-Border-Wall.pdf.

16 Scott Nicol, "New Border Walls Designed to Flood Texas Towns," *The Texas Observer*, July 11, 2012, https://www.texasobserver.org/new-border-walls -designed-to-flood-texas-towns/.

17 John Burnett, "Mexico Worries That A New Border Wall Will Worsen Flooding," NPR, April 25, 2017, accessed May 31, 2018, https://www.npr. org/2017/04/25/525383494/trump-s-proposed-u-s-mexico-border-wall-may -violate-1970-treaty.

18 Ibid.

19 Jesse R. Lasky, Walter Jetz, and Timothy H. Keitt, "Conservation Biogeography of the US-Mexico Border: A Transcontinental Risk Assessment of Barriers to Animal Dispersal," *Diversity and Distributions* 17, no. 4 (2011): 673-687, doi:10.1111/j.1472-4642.2011.00765.x.

20 Jacob Soboroff, "House Bill Bans Border Wall Construction in Federal Wildlife Refuge," NBCNews.com, March 22, 2018, https://www.nbcnews.com/politics/ national-security/house-bill-bans-border-wall-construction-santa-ana-wildlife- refuge-n859191.

21 Nash Jenkins, "Trump Got $1.6 Billion For Border Security. He Says It Isn't Enough," *Time*, March 22, 2018, http://time.com/5210780/congress-omnibus -border-security-wall-donald-trump/.

22 Tal Kopan, Rene Marsh, and Gregory Wallace, "Trump Admin Waives Laws for Border Wall," CNN, August 2, 2017, https://www.cnn.com/2017/08/01/politics/ trump-waives-environmental-laws-border-wall/index.html.

23 Wes Siler, "These Are the 111 Endangered Species Threatened by Trump's Wall," Outside Online, May 23, 2017, https://www.outsideonline.com/2075761/trumps -wall-threatens-111-endangered-species.

24 Noah Greenwald et al., "A Wall in the Wild: The Disastrous Impact of Trump's Border Wall on Wildlife," May 2017, 1–17, http://www.biologicaldiversity.org/ programs/ international/borderlands_and_boundary_waters/ pdfs/ A_Wall_in _the_Wild.pdf.

25 Shanika Gunaratna, "Trump's Border Wall Would Be 'Catastrophe' for Wildlife, Expert Says," CBS News, March 29, 2017, https://www.cbsnews.com/news/trump-mexican-border-wall-environmental-wildlife-catastrophe/.

26 Eliza Barclay, "Congress Is Quietly Letting Trump Bulldoze a Butterfly Refuge to Build a Border Wall," Vox, March 28, 2018, https://www.vox.com/2018/3/28/17152644/trump-border-wall-texas-environment-refuge-butterflies.

27 Kyle Woosnam et al., "An Initial Examination of the Economic Impact of Nature...," US Fish and Wildlife Service, September 1, 2011, i–11, https://www.fws.gov/uploadedfiles/naturereport-mcallencvb-2011_508.pdf.

28 Eliza Barclay, "Congress Is Quietly Letting Trump Bulldoze a Butterfly Refuge to Build a Border Wall," Vox, March 28, 2018, https://www.vox.com/2018/3/28/17152644/trump-border-wall-texas-environment-refuge-butterflies.

29 "Border Wall Information," National Butterfly Center, https://www.nationalbutterflycenter.org/about-nbc/maps-directions/9-national-butterfly-center/258-border-wall-information.

30 Melissa del Bosque, "National Butterfly Center Sues Trump Administration Over Border Wall," The Texas Observer, December 12, 2017, https://www.texasobserver.org/national-butterfly-center-sues-trump-administration-border-wall/.

31 Cally Carswell, "Trump's Wall May Threaten Thousands of Plant and Animal Species on the US-Mexico Border," Scientific American, May 10, 2017. https://www.scientificamerican.com/article/trump-rsquo-s-wall-may-threaten-thousands-of-plant-and-animal-species-on-the-u-s-mexico-border/.

32 Ibid.

33 "Environmental Laws Waived for Border Fence," NBCNews.com, October 23, 2007, http://www.nbcnews.com/id/21432742/ns/us_news-environment/t/environmental-laws-waived-border-fence/#.WujnEojwY2w.

34 US Department of Homeland Security, "DHS Issues Waiver to Expedite Border Construction Projects in San Diego Area," News Release, August 1, 2017, Homeland Security, https://www.dhs.gov/news/2017/08/01/dhs-issues-waiver-expedite-border-construction-projects-san-diego-area.

35 Geneva Sands, "Judge, Once Berated by Trump, Rules in Favor of Border Wall Waivers," ABC News, February 28, 2018, http://abcnews.go.com/Politics/judge-berated-trump-rules-favor-border-wall-waivers/story?id=53427234.

36 Jacqueline Thomsen, "Mexican-American Judge Who Trump Attacked Rules in Favor of Border Wall," The Hill, February 28, 2018, http://thehill.com/regulation/court-battles/375875-mexican-american-judge-that-trump-attacked-rules-in-favor-of-trumps.

37 Tal Kopan, Rene Marsh, and Gregory Wallace, "Trump Admin Waives Laws for Border Wall," CNN, August 02, 2017, https://www.cnn.com/2017/08/01/politics/trump-waives-environmental-laws-border-wall/index.html.

38 Tal Kopan, "Report: Trump Admin Taking Steps on Seizing Border Land," CNN, November 14, 2017, https://www.cnn.com/2017/11/13/politics/border-wall-eminent-domain/index.html.

39 Chris Ramirez and John C. Moritz, "Border Homes, and the Wall That Would Tear Them Apart," USA Today, n.d., https://www.usatoday.com/border-wall/story/eminent-domain-trump-border-wall-rio-grande/638916001/.

40 Ibid.

41 Dianna M. Náñez, "Tohono O'odham Tribal Members Opposing Trump's Border Wall Take Fight to McCain," Azcentral, March 24, 2017, https://www.azcentral.com/story/news/politics/border-issues/2017/03/23/tohono-oodham-trump-border-wall/99550594/.

42 Dianna M. Náñez, "A Border Tribe, and the Wall That Will Divide It," USA Today, accessed May 31, 2018, https://www.usatoday.com/border-wall/story/tohono-oodham-nation-arizona-tribe/582487001/. Jose Pancho, "Tohono O'odham-English Dictionary," 1–455, n.d., http://www.acsu.buffalo.edu/~mathiotm/Mathiot/Volume%20I.pdf

43 Rick LoBello, "Coalition Renews Big Bend International Park Campaign," Rio Grande Chapter, October 25, 2016, http://www.riograndesierraclub.org/coalition-renews-big-bend-international-park-campaign/.

44 Eryn Gable, "75 Years On, Effort to Create US-Mexico Park Hampered by Security Concerns," The New York Times, June 24, 2010, https://archive.nytimes.com/www.nytimes.com/gwire/2010/06/24/24greenwire-75-years-on-effort-to-create-us-mexico-park-ha-13949.html.

45 Jason Abrams, "Timeline," Greater Big Bend Coalition, November 17, 2017, https://greaterbigbend.wordpress.com/ international-park-timeline-2/.

46 Gabriel Diaz Montemayor, "Here's a Better Vision for the US-Mexico Border: Make the Rio Grande Grand Again," The Conversation, August 22, 2017, http://theconversation.com/heres-a-better-vision-for-the-us-mexico-border-make-the-rio-grande-grand-again-73111.

47 Joe Sirotnak, "Binational Cooperation in the Big Bend Region," The George Wright Forum 28, no. 3 (2011): 291–295, http://www.georgewright.org/283sirotnak.pdf.

48 "Partners in Protection of the Chihuahuan Desert," National Parks Service, February 24, 2015, https:// www.nps.gov/bibe/learn/nature/mexareas.htm.

49 US Department of the Interior, Big Bend National Park, "Secretaries Jewell, Guerra Celebrate the Binational Big Bend/Río Bravo Conservation Partnership, Two-Year Anniversary of Boquillas Port of Entry," News Release, October 4, 2015, https://www.doi.gov/news/pressreleases/secretaries-jewell-guerra-celebrate-the -binational-big-bend-rio-bravo-conservation-partnership-two-year -anniversary-of-boquillas-port-of-entry.

50 Eryn Gable, "75 Years On, Effort to Create US-Mexico Park Hampered by Security Concerns," The New York Times, June 24, 2010, https://archive.nytimes. com/www.nytimes.com/gwire/2010/06/24/24greenwire-75-years-on-effort-to -create-us-mexico-park-ha-13949.html.

51 Ibid.

Chapter 3: Brick by Brick

1 Ylarregui José Salazar, Datos de los Trabajos Astronómicos y Topográficos, Dispuestos en Forma de Diario: Practicados Durante el año de 1849 y Principios de 1850 por la...la de los Estados-Unidos (Mexico:Impr. de J. R. Navarro, 1850), 36, in Rachel St. John, Line in the Sand: A History of the Western US-Mexico Border, Kindle ed. (Princeton: Princeton University Press, 2011), 11.

2 "Notable Quotes of Sam Houston," Sam Houston Memorial Museum, accessed May 31, 2018, http://samhouston memorialmuseum.com/history/quotes.html.

3 Garon Blazeski, "Pancho Villa Is Reported to Have Died Saying, 'Don't Let It End like This. Tell Them I Said Something,'" The Vintage News, July 15, 2017, https://www.thevintagenews.com/2017/07/16/pancho-villa-is-reported-to-have- died-saying-dont-let-it-end-like-this-tell-them-i-said-something/.

4 Ron Dungan, "A Moving Border, and the History of a Difficult Boundary," USA Today, accessed May 31, 2018, https://www.usatoday.com/border-wall/story/us -mexico-border-history/510833001/.

5 "The Adams-Onis Treaty of 1819," Sons of Dewittt Colony Texas, accessed May 31, 2018, http://www.sonsofdewittcolony.org/adamonis.htm.

6 CFR, "Timeline: US-Mexico Relations," Council on Foreign Relations, accessed May 31, 2018, https://www.cfr.org/ timeline/us-mexico-relations.

7   Ron Dungan, "A Moving Border, and the History of a Difficult Boundary," *USA Today*, accessed May 31, 2018, https://www.usatoday.com/border-wall /story/us-mexico-border-history/510833001/.

8   "Articles of the Decree of April 1830," The Portal to Texas History, accessed May 31, 2018, https://education.texashistory.unt.edu/lessons/notebook/LawApril /docs/LawApril_Articles.pdf.

9   Jay Root, "When Americans Were Illegal Immigrants in Mexico," *The New York Times*, December 13, 2012, https://www.nytimes.com/2012/12/14/us/when -americans-were-illegal-immigrants-in-mexico.html.

10 CFR, "Timeline: US-Mexico Relations," Council on Foreign Relations, accessed May 31, 2018, https://www.cfr.org/ timeline/us-mexico-relations.

11 Rachel St. John, *Line in the Sand: A History of the Western US-Mexico Border*, Kindle ed. (Princeton: Princeton University Press, 2011), 2.

12 Ibid.

13 "Gadsden Purchase, 1853–1854," US Department of State, accessed May 31, 2018, https://history.state.gov/ milestones/1830-1860/gadsden-purchase.

14 Rachel St. John, *Line in the Sand: A History of the Western US-Mexico Border*, Kindle ed. (Princeton: Princeton University Press, 2011), 1.

15 Rachel St. John, *Line in the Sand: A History of the Western US-Mexico Border*, Kindle ed. (Princeton: Princeton University Press, 2011), 90.

16 Rachel St. John, *Line in the Sand: A History of the Western US-Mexico Border*, Kindle ed. (Princeton: Princeton University Press, 2011), 105.

17 Ibid.

18 Rachel St. John, *Line in the Sand: A History of the Western US-Mexico Border*, Kindle ed. (Princeton: Princeton University Press, 2011), 122.

19 Rachel St. John. *Bridging National Borders in North America.* A. R. Benjamin H. Johnson, ed. (Durham and London: Duke University Press, 2010), 116.

20 Rachel St. John, *Line in the Sand: A History of the Western US-Mexico Border*, Kindle ed. (Princeton: Princeton University Press, 2011), 203.

21 "Southwest Borderlands," National Museum of American History, May 3, 2018, http://americanhistory.si.edu/many-voices-exhibition/new-americans -continuing-debates-1965–2000/southwest-borderlands.

22 Rachel St. John, *Line in the Sand: A History of the Western US-Mexico Border*, Kindle ed. (Princeton: Princeton University Press, 2011), 204.

23 "Border Patrol History," US Customs and Border Protection, March 24, 2018, https://www.cbp.gov/border-security/along-us-borders/history.

24 David Bier, "Why the Wall Won't Work," Cato Institute, April 10, 2017, https://www.cato.org/ publications/ commentary/why-wall-wont-work.

25 David Stout, "Bush Signs Bill Ordering Fence on Mexican Border," *The New York Times*, October 26, 2006, https:// www.nytimes.com/2006/10/26/washington/27fencecnd.html.

26 "Fact Sheet: The Secure Fence Act of 2006," The White House, October 26, 2016, https://georgewbush-whitehouse. archives.gov/news/releases/2006/10/20061026-1.html.

27 R. Rael, "Boundary Line Infrastructure," *Thresholds* 20 (2012):75–82.

28 David Stout, "Bush Signs Bill Ordering Fence on Mexican Border," *The New York Times*, October 26, 2006, https:// www.nytimes.com/2006/10/26/washington/27fencecnd.html.

29 Rachel St. John, *Line in the Sand: A History of the Western US-Mexico Border*, Kindle ed. (Princeton: Princeton University Press, 2011), 205.

30 Estimates vary. According to the Government Accountability office, the border runs 1,954 miles. US Customs and Border Protection lists 1,900 miles. More information here: https://www.azcentral.com/story/news/politics/border-issues/2017/09/23/how-long-u-s-mexico-border/697411001/

31 David Ingold et al., "Trump's Wall with Mexico: What We Know," Bloomberg, February 13, 2017, https://www.bloomberg.com/graphics/2017-trump-mexico-wall/how-many-people-currently-cross/.

32 "The Wall—An In-depth Examination of Donald Trump's Border Wall," *USA Today*, accessed May 31, 2018, https://www.usatoday.com/border-wall/.

33 David Ingold et al., "Trump's Wall with Mexico: What We Know," Bloomberg, February 13, 2017, https://www.bloomberg.com/graphics/2017-trump-mexico-wall/how-many-people-currently-cross/.

34 Vanda Felbab-Brown, "The Wall: The Real Costs of a Barrier between the United States and Mexico," Brookings, September 15, 2017, https://www.brookings.edu/essay/the-wall-the-real-costs-of-a-barrier-between-the-united-states-and-mexico/#price-tag.

35 "Here's What We Know About Trump's Mexico Wall." Bloomberg. February 13, 2013. https://www.bloomberg.com/graphics/2017-trump-mexico-wall/how-long-would-the-wall-be/.

Chapter 4: The Mental Dam

1 Timothy B. Tyson, "The Civil Rights Stories We Need to Remember," *The New York Times*, May 19, 2017, https://www.nytimes.com/2017/05/19/books/review/he-calls-me-by-lightning-s-jonathan-bass.html.

2 Original quote is in J. E. Dougherty, *Illegals: The Imminent Threat Posed by Our Unsecured US–Mexico Border* (Nashville, TN: Thomas Nelson, 2004), cited in M. Stein, *American Panic: A History of Who Scares Us and Why,* (New York: St. Martin's Press, 2014), 197.

3 Andrew Paxman, *Jenkins of Mexico: How a Southern Farm Boy Became a Mexican Magnate* (New York: Oxford University Press, 2017), 61.

4 AMLO, "Speech by AMLO in Los Angeles, California" (speech, Plaza Olvera, Los Angeles, February 12, 2017), https://lopezobrador.org.mx/2017/02/12/speech-by-amlo-in-los-angeles-california/.

5 Ibid.

6 Luis Gomez, "Meet the Mexican Presidential Hopeful Who Campaigned in California," Sandiegouniontribune.com, March 9, 2018, http://www.sandiegouniontribune.com/opinion/the-conversation/sd-mexican-presidential-candidate-ricardo-anaya-campaign-california-20180309-htmlstory.html.

7 "José Antonio Meade Secunda a Peña Nieto Y Le Pide Respeto a Donald Trump," *Expansión*, April 6, 2018, https://expansion.mx/video-politica/2018/04/06/jose-antonio-meade-secunda-a-pena-nieto-y-le-pide-respeto-a-donald-trump.

8 Adam Taylor, "Mexican Views of the United States Drop to Record Low, Poll Finds," *The Washington Post*, January 18, 2018, https://www.washingtonpost.com/news/worldviews/wp/2018/01/18/mexican-views-of-the-united-states-drop-to-record-low-poll-finds/?utm_term=.1db58b2fb0a3.

9 Will Worley, "Mexicans Celebrate Easter by Blowing up Effigy of Donald Trump," *The Independent*, April 17, 2017, https://www.independent.co.uk/news/world/americas/mexico-city-burns-effigy-donald-trump-judas-iscariot-celebrate-easter-a7687701.html.

10 John Lee Anderson, "How Mexico Deals with Trump," *The New Yorker,* May 31, 2018, https://www.newyorker.com/magazine/2017/10/09/mexico-in-the-age-of-trump.

11 Ronald R. Sundstrom, "Sheltering Xenophobia," *Critical Philosophy of Race* 1, no. 1 (2013): 68–85, doi:10.5325/critphilrace.1.1.0068.

12 Andrea Navarro, "Starbucks Sales at Mexico's Alsea Hit by Anti-Trump Sentiment," Bloomberg, April 27, 2017, https://www.bloomberg.com/news/articles/2017-04-27/starbucks-sales-at-mexico-s-alsea-hit-by-anti-trump-sentiment.

13 Frederick C. Turner, "Anti-Americanism in Mexico, 1910–1913," *The Hispanic American Historical Review* 47, no. 4 (November 1967): 502–18.

14 Ibid.

15 Frederick C. Turner, *The Dynamic of Mexican Nationalism* (University of North Carolina Press, 1968), 212.

16 Frederick C. Turner, "Anti-Americanism in Mexico, 1910–1913," *The Hispanic American Historical Review* 47, no. 4 (November 1967): 502–18.

17 Ibid.

18 Andrew Paxman, "The Return of Gringophobia," *Slate* magazine, May 29, 2017, http://www.slate.com/articles/news_and_politics/foreigners/2017/05/what_the_history_of_mexican_anti_americanism_can_tell_us_about_the_trump.html.

19 Saladin Ambar, "Woodrow Wilson: Foreign Affairs," Miller Center, accessed May 31, 2018, https://millercenter.org/ president/wilson/foreign-affairs.

20 Ibid.

21 Peter V. N. Henderson, "Woodrow Wilson, Victoriano Huerta, and the Recognition Issue in Mexico," *The Americas* 41, no. 2 (1984): 151–76.

22 Ibid.

23 Frederick C. Turner, "Anti-Americanism in Mexico, 1910–1913," *The Hispanic American Historical Review* 47, no. 4 (November 1967): 502–518.

24 Enrique Krauze, "The April Invasion of Veracruz," *The New York Times*, April 20, 2014. https://www.nytimes.com/2014/04/21/opinion/krauze-the-april-invasion-of-veracruz.html.

25 Guadalupe San Miguel Jr., *Brown, Not White: School Integration and the Chicano Movement in Houston* (College Station: Texas A&M University Press, 2005).

26 Mark Stein, *American Panic: A History of Who Scares Us and Why* (New York: St. Martin's Press, 2014). 198.

27 Ibid.

28 Mark Stein, *American Panic: A History of Who Scares Us and Why* (New York: St. Martin's Press, 2014). 201.

29 Mark Stein, *American Panic: A History of Who Scares Us and Why* (New York: St. Martin's Press, 2014). 202.

30 William D. Carrigan and Clive Webb, *Forgotten Dead: Mob Violence against Mexicans in the United States, 1848–1928* (New York: Oxford University Press, 2013), 143–45.

31 Ibid.

32 William D. Carrigan and Clive Webb, *Forgotten Dead: Mob Violence against Mexicans in the United States, 1848–1928* (New York: Oxford University Press, 2013), appendix.

33 William Carrigan, "The History of Anti-Mexican Violence And Lynching." NPR (podcast), March 17, 2017. https://www.npr.org/2017/03/17/520576256/the-history-of-anti-mexican-violence-and-lynching.

34 William D. Carrigan and Clive Webb, *Forgotten Dead: Mob Violence against Mexicans in the United States, 1848–1928* (New York: Oxford University Press, 2013), 20–25.

35 William D. Carrigan and Clive Webb, "The Lynching of Persons of Mexican Origin or Descent in the United States, 1848–1928." *Journal of Social History,* 37, no. 2 (2003): 411–38.

Chapter 5: The Walls Came Tumbling Down

1   "Mexicans Returning Home Outnumber Those Immigrating to US, Study Shows," *The Guardian*, November 19, 2015, https://www.theguardian.com/us-news/2015/nov/19/mexicans-returning-home-outnumber-those-immigrating-to-us-study-shows.

2   Carlos Salinas de Gortari, "Salinas Speaks Out On Free Trade In an Exclusive Interview, Mexico's President Rebuffs Naysayers on NAFTA and Argues That the Agreement Will Produce Winners on Both Sides of the Rio Grande. He Knows His Economics," December 28, 1992, *Fortune Magazine*, http://archive.fortune.com/magazines/fortune/fortune_archive/1992/12/28/77310/index.htm.

3   Clinton, William J. "William J. Clinton: Remarks at the Signing Ceremony for the Supplemental Agreements to the North American Free Trade Agreement—September 14, 1993," The American Presidency Project, September 14, 1993, http://www.presidency.ucsb.edu/ws/?pid=47070.

4   Antonio Flores, "How the US Hispanic Population Is Changing," Pew Research Center, September 18, 2017, http://www.pewresearch.org/fact-tank/2017/09/18/how-the-u-s-hispanic-population-is-changing/.

5   Ibid.

6   "Hispanics in the US Fast Facts," CNN, March 22, 2018, https://www.cnn.com/2013/09/20/us/hispanics-in-the-u-s-/index.html.

7   Ibid.

8   William H. Frey, "The US Will Become 'Minority White' in 2045, Census Projects," Brookings, March 14, 2018, https://www.brookings.edu/blog/the-avenue/2018/03/14/the-us-will-become-minority-white-in-2045-census-projects/.

9   Mark Hugo Lopez, "In 2014, Latinos will surpass whites as largest racial/ethnic group in California," Pew Research Center, January 24, 2014, http://www.pewresearch.org/fact-tank/2014/01/24/in-2014-latinos-will-surpass-whites-as-largest-racialethnic-group-in-california/.

10   Alex Seitz-Wald, "Actually, Salsa Dethroned Ketchup 20 Years Ago," The Atlantic, October 17, 2013, https://www.theatlantic.com/national/archive/2013/10/actually-salsa-dethroned-ketchup-20-years-ago/309844/.

11   Antonio Flores, "How the US Hispanic Population Is Changing," Pew Research Center, September 18, 2017, http://www.pewresearch.org/fact-tank/2017/09/18/how-the-u-s-hispanic-population-is-changing/.

12   Gustavo López, "Hispanics of Mexican Origin in the United States, 2013," Pew Research Center's Hispanic Trends Project, September 15, 2015, http://www.pewhispanic.org/2015/09/15/hispanics-of-mexican-origin-in-the-united-states-2013/.

13   Emma Aguila et al., United States and Mexico: Ties That Bind, Issues That Divide (Santa Monica: RAND Corporation, 2012).

14   Jie Zong and Jeanne Batalova, "Mexican Immigrants in the United States," Migrationpolicy.org, March 02, 2017, https://www.migrationpolicy.org/article/mexican-immigrants-united-states.

15   "Mexicans Returning Home Outnumber Those Immigrating to US, Study Shows," The Guardian, November 19, 2015, https://www.theguardian.com/us-news/2015/nov/19/mexicans-returning-home-outnumber-those-immigrating-to-us-study-shows.

16   Jie Zong and Jeanne Batalova, "Mexican Immigrants in the United States," Migrationpolicy.org, March 17, 2016, https://www.migrationpolicy.org/article/mexican-immigrants-united-states#Income and Poverty.

17   Serena Marshall, "Obama Has Deported More People Than Any Other President," ABC News, August 29, 2016, http://abcnews.go.com/Politics/obamas-deportation-policy-numbers/story?id=41715661.

18   Muzaffar Chishti et al., "The Obama Record on Deportations: Deporter in Chief or Not?" Migrationpolicy.org, March 22, 2017, accessed May 31, 2018, https://www.migrationpolicy.org/article/obama-record-deportations-deporter-chief-or-not.

19   Filiz Garip, "Discovering Diverse Mechanisms of Migration: The Mexico-US Stream 1970–2000," *Population and Development Review* 38, no. 3 (2012): 393–433.

20   Jens Manuel Krogstad, Jeffrey S. Passel, and D'Vera Cohn, "5 Facts about Illegal Immigration in the US," Pew Research Center, April 27, 2017, http://www.pewresearch.org/fact-tank/2017/04/27/5-facts-about-illegal-immigration-in-the -u-s/.

21   Ibid.

22   Vivian Yee, Kenan Davis, and Jugal K. Patel, "Here's the Reality About Illegal Immigrants in the United States," *The New York Times*, March 6, 2017, https://www.nytimes.com/interactive/2017/03/06/us/politics/undocumented-illegal -immigrants.html.

23   Laura Mallonee, "Wanna See How Divided the Country Is? Visit the US-Mexico Border," *Wired*, August 24, 2017, https://www.wired.com/story/wanna-see-how -divided-the-country-is-visit-the-us-mexico-border/.

24   Ana Gonzalez-Barrera and Jens Manuel Krogstad, "What We Know about Illegal Immigration from Mexico," Pew Research Center, March 2, 2017, http://www.pewresearch.org/fact-tank/2017/03/02/what-we-know-about-illegal -immigration-from-mexico/.

25   "Here's What We Know About Trump's Mexico Wall," Bloomberg, February 13, 2013, https://www.bloomberg.com/graphics/2017-trump-mexico-wall/how-long-would -the-wall-be/.

26   Ana Gonzalez-Barrera and Jens Manuel Krogstad, "What We Know about Illegal Immigration from Mexico," Pew Research Center, March 2, 2017, http://www.pewresearch.org/fact-tank/2017/03/02/what-we-know-about-illegal -immigration-from-mexico/.

27   John Burnett, "Arrests For Illegal Border Crossings Hit 46-Year Low," National Public Radio (NPR), December 5, 2017, https://www.npr.org/2017/12/05/568546381 /arrests-for-illegal-border-crossings-hit-46-year-low.

28   Gustavo Solis, "Drug Smuggling, and the Endless Battle to Stop It," *USA Today*, accessed May 31, 2018, https://www.usatoday.com/border-wall/story/drug -trafficking-smuggling-cartels-tunnels/559814001/.

29   Ibid

30   Ibid.

31 Ron Nixon, "By Land, Sea or Catapult: How Smugglers Get Drugs Across the Border," *The New York Times*, July 25, 2017, https://www.nytimes.com/2017/07/25/us/drugs-border-wall.html.

32 Eugene Kiely, "Fact Check: Will President Trump's Border Wall Stop Drug Smuggling?" *USA Today*, August 31, 2017, https://www.usatoday.com/story/news/politics/2017/08/31/fact-check-president-trump-border-wall-drug-smuggling/619865001/.

33 "How Do Cartels Get Drugs into the US?" BBC News, December 3, 2015, http://www.bbc.com/news/world-us-canada-34934574.

34 Homeland Security, "US-Mexico Bi-National Criminal Proceeds Study," ICE, accessed May 31, 2018, https://www.ice.gov/doclib/cornerstone/pdf/cps-study.pdf.

35 Ron Nixon and Fernanda Santos, "US Appetite for Mexico's Drugs Fuels Illegal Immigration," *The New York Times*, April 5, 2017, https://www.nytimes.com/2017/04/04/us/politics/us-appetite-for-mexicos-drugs-fuels-illegal-immigration.html.

36 GAO, "Firearms Trafficking: US Efforts to Combat Firearms Trafficking to Mexico Have Improved, but Some Collaboration Challenges Remain," US Government Accountability Office (US GAO), January 11, 2016, https://www.gao.gov/products/GAO-16-223.

37 "Mexico Drug War Fast Facts," CNN, March 21, 2018, https://www.cnn.com/2013/09/02/world/americas/mexico-drug-war-fast-facts/index.html.

Paulina Villegas, "Missing Mexicans' Case Shines Light on Military's Role in Drug War," *The New York Times*, April 30, 2018, https://www.nytimes.com/2018/04/30/world/americas/mexico-missing-military-drugs.html.

38 Max Fisher and Amanda Taub, "Mexico's Record Violence Is a Crisis 20 Years in the Making," *The New York Times*, October 28, 2017, https://www.nytimes.com/2017/10/28/world/americas/mexico-violence.html.

39 Jonaki Bose et al., "Key Substance Use and Mental Health Indicators in the United States: Results From the 2015 National Survey on Drug Use and Health," Substance Abuse and Mental Health Service Administration (SAMHSA), September 2016, 1–43, https://www.samhsa.gov/data/sites/default/files/NSDUH-FFR1-2015/NSDUH-FFR1-2015/NSDUH-FFR1-2015.pdf.

40 German Lopez, "In One Year, Drug Overdoses Killed More Americans than the Entire Vietnam War Did," Vox, June 06, 2017, https://www.vox.com/policy-and-politics/2017/6/6/15743986/opioid-epidemic-overdose-deaths-2016.

41 "Sociocultural Dimensions of Immigrant Integration," in *The Integration of Immigrants into American Society*, ed. Mary C. Waters and Marisa Gerstein

Pineau (Washington, DC: National Academies Press, 2015), 303–44, https://www.nap.edu/read/21746/chapter/9#325.

42 Ibid.

43 Michelangelo Landgrave and Alex Nowrasteh, "Criminal Immigrants: Their Numbers, Demographics, and Countries of Origin," Cato Institute, March 15, 2017, https://www.cato.org/publications/immigration-reform-bulletin/criminal-immigrants-their-numbers-demographics-countries.

44 Vivian Yee, Kenan Davis, and Jugal K. Patel, "Here's the Reality About Illegal Immigrants in the United States," *The New York Times*, March 6, 2017, https://www.nytimes.com/interactive/2017/03/06/us/politics/undocumented-illegal-immigrants.html.

45 Vanda Felbab-Brown, "The Wall: The Real Costs of a Barrier between the United States and Mexico," Brookings, September 15, 2017, https://www.brookings.edu/essay/the-wall-the-real-costs-of-a-barrier-between-the-united-states-and-mexico/#economy

46 Michelle Ye Hee Lee, "Analysis | Donald Trump's False Comments Connecting Mexican Immigrants and Crime," *The Washington Post*. July 8, 2015, accessed May 31, 2018, https://www.washingtonpost.com/news/fact-checker/wp/2015/07/08/donald-trumps-false-comments-connecting-mexican-immigrants-and-crime/?noredirect=on&utm_term=.6c671c95bcf0.

47 W.W. "Blame Mexico!" *The Economist*, August 18, 2015, https://www.economist.com/blogs/democracyinamerica/2015/08/donald-trump-immigration-reform.

48 Anna Flagg, "The Myth of the Criminal Immigrant," *The New York Times*, March 30, 2018, https://www.nytimes.com/interactive/2018/03/30/upshot/crime-immigration-myth.html.

49 Dennis Wagner, "Border Violence, and the Families in Its Wake," *USA Today*, accessed May 31, 2018, https://www.usatoday.com/border-wall/story/brian-terry-us-border-patrol-agent/560448001/.

50 *Criminal Alien Statistics Information on Incarcerations, Arrests, and Costs*, report no. GAO-11-187, United States Government Accountability Office, March 2011, https://www.gao.gov/assets/320/316959.pdf.

51 David Bier, "Why the Wall Won't Work," Cato Institute, April 10, 2017, https://www.cato.org/publications/commentary/why-wall-wont-work.

52 Vivian Yee, Kenan Davis, and Jugal K. Patel, "Here's the Reality About Illegal Immigrants in the United States," *The New York Times*, March 6, 2017, https://www.nytimes.com/interactive/2017/03/06/us/politics/undocumented-illegal-immigrants.html

53 "Here's What We Know About Trump's Mexico Wall," Bloomberg, February 13, 2013, https://www.bloomberg.com/graphics/2017-trump-mexico-wall/how-long -would-the-wall-be/.

54 David Inserra, "The Wall Is Not Enough. Here's How to Solve Illegal Immigration," The Heritage Foundation, January 9, 2018, https://www.heritage.org/immigration /commentary/the-wall-not-enough-heres-how-solve-illegal-immigration.

55 Ioan Grillo, "Mexican Drug Smugglers to Trump: Thanks!" *The New York Times*, May 5, 2017, https://www.nytimes.com/2017/05/05/opinion/sunday/mexican -drug-smugglers-to-trump-thanks.html?_r=0.

56 David Bier, "Why the Wall Won't Work," Cato Institute, April 10, 2017, https:// www.cato.org/publications/commentary/why-wall-wont-work.

57 "Mexico 'Will Not Pay for US Border Wall'—President Enrique Pena Nieto," BBC News, January 26, 2017, http://www.bbc.com/news/av/world-latin-america-38753660/ mexico-will-not-pay-for-us-border-wall-president-enrique-pena-nieto.

58 Vanda Felbab-Brown, "The Wall: The Real Costs of a Barrier between the United States and Mexico," Brookings, September 15, 2017, https://www.brookings. edu/essay/the-wall-the-real-costs-of-a-barrier-between-the-united-states-and -mexico/#economy

59 Ibid.

60 Reid J. Epstein, "Ga. Immigrant Crackdown Backfires," June 22, 2011, *Politico*, https:// www.politico.com/story/2011/06/ga-immigrant-crackdown-backfires-057551.

61 Rick Barrett, "Dairy Farms Fear Trump's Immigration Policies," *Milwaukee Journal Sentinel*, March 7, 2017, https://www.jsonline.com/story/money/ business/2017/03/06/dairy-farms-fear-trumps-immigration-policies/98700808/

62 Maria E. Enchautegui, "Immigrant and Native Workers Compete for Different Low-skilled Jobs," Urban Institute, March 25, 2016, https://www.urban.org/ urban-wire/immigrant-and-native-workers-compete-different-low-skilled-jobs.

63 Vanda Felbab-Brown, "The Wall: The Real Costs of a Barrier between the United States and Mexico," Brookings, September 15, 2017, https://www.brookings. edu/essay/the-wall-the-real-costs-of-a-barrier-between-the-united-states-and -mexico/#price-tag.

64 Paul Davidson, "Automation Could Kill 73 Million US Jobs by 2030," *USA Today*, November 29, 2017, https://www.usatoday.com/story/money/2017/11/29 /automation-could-kill-73-million-u-s-jobs-2030/899878001/.

65 M. Angeles Villarreal and Ian F. Fergusson, "The North American Free Trade Agreement (NAFTA)," FAS. May 24, 2017, https://fas.org/sgp/crs/row/R42965.pdf.

66 Paul Krugman, "The Uncomfortable Truth about NAFTA: Its Foreign Policy, Stupid," *Foreign Affairs* 72, no. 5 (1993): 13–19.

67 James McBride and Mohammed Aly Sergie, "NAFTA's Economic Impact," Council on Foreign Relations, https://www.cfr.org/backgrounder/naftas-economic-impact.

68 Ibid.

69 "What if NAFTA breaks up?" HSBC Global Research, November 16, 2017.

70 James McBride and Mohammed Aly Sergie, "NAFTA's Economic Impact," Council on Foreign Relations, https://www.cfr.org/backgrounder/naftas-economic-impact.

71 John Kingston, "The Economic Impact of NAFTA—Frequently Asked Questions," S&P Global Market Intelligence, January 10, 2018, https://www.spglobal.com /our-insights/FAQ-The-Economic-Impact-of-NAFTA.html.

72 Kristina Johnson and Samuel Fromartz, "NAFTA's 'Broken Promises': These Farmers Say They Got The Raw End Of Trade Deal," NPR, August 07, 2017, https://www.npr.org/sections/thesalt/2017/08/07/541671747/nafta-s-broken-promises-these-farmers-say-they-got-the-raw-end-of-trade-deal.

73 James McBride and Mohammed Aly Sergie, "NAFTA's Economic Impact," Council on Foreign Relations, https://www.cfr.org/backgrounder/naftas-economic-impact.

74 Ibid.

75 Kimberly Amadeo, "Why NAFTA's Six Advantages Outweigh Its Six Disadvantages," *The Balance*, March 6, 2018, https://www.thebalance.com/nafta-pros-and-cons-3970481.

76 Robbie Whelan and Santiago Pérez, "Why Your Flat-Screen TV Would Cost More If NAFTA Ends," *The Wall Street Journal*, November 27, 2017, https://www.wsj.com/ articles/why-your-flat-screen-tv-would-cost-more-if-nafta-ends-1511344800.

77 M. Angeles Villarreal and Ian F. Fergusson, The North American Free Trade Agreement (NAFTA), report no. R42965, Congressional Research Service, May 24, 2017, 1–38, https://fas.org/sgp/crs/row/R42965.pdf.

78 "Ready to Take off Again?" *The Economist*, January 4, 2014, https://www. economist.com/news/briefing/21592631-two-decades-ago-north-american -free-trade-agreement-got-flying-start-then-it.

79 Michael Clemens, "The US-Mexico Wage Gap Has Grown, Not Shrunk, under NAFTA. Awkward," Center For Global Development, March 17, 2015, https:// www.cgdev.org/blog/us-mexico-wage-gap-has-grown-not-shrunk-under-nafta -awkward.

80 "What if NAFTA breaks up?" HSBC Global Research, November 16, 2017.

Notes

81 Gary Hufbauer, Cathleen Cimino, and Tyler Moran, "NAFTA at 20: Misleading Charges and Positive Achievements," PIIE, May 2014, 1–22, https://piie.com/sites/default/files/publications/pb/pb14-13.pdf.

82 WSDBHome, accessed June 1, 2018, http://stat.wto.org/TariffProfiles/MX_e.htm.

83 Blake Hurst, "A Farmer's View of NAFTA," *National Review*, October 26, 2017, https://www.nationalreview.com/2017/10/nafta-farmers-case-trade-deal/.

84 USDA, "Infographic: US Agricultural Exports to Mexico, 2016," CAFTA-DR: A Trade Partnership That Works | USDA Foreign Agricultural Service, May 5, 2017, https://www.fas.usda.gov/data/infographic-us-agricultural-exports-mexico-2016.

85 Kingston, John. "The Economic Impact of NAFTA—Frequently Asked Questions." S&P Global Market Intelligence. January 10, 2018. https://www.spglobal.com/our-insights/FAQ-The-Economic-Impact-of-NAFTA.html.

86 Shannon K. O'Neil, *Two Nations Indivisible Mexico, the United States, and the Road Ahead* (New York: Oxford University Press, 2015), 4.

87 John Kingston, "The Economic Impact of NAFTA—Frequently Asked Questions," S&P Global Market Intelligence, January 10, 2018, https://www.spglobal.com/our-insights/FAQ-The-Economic-Impact-of-NAFTA.html.

Ana Tijoux delivers an electrifying rap during the New York sessions